Laura G. Manis

WOMANPOWER

A manual for workshops in personal effectiveness

THE CARROLL PRESS
Publishers
CRANSTON, R.I. 02920

About the Author –

LAURA G. MANIS has been a counselor at Western Michigan University for the past ten years. Her special interest is in working with women by developing programs which meet their special needs. She helped plan and establish the Department of Continuing Education for Women and set up the Susan B. Anthony Center, a campus women's center and outreach program. She also established and coordinates the Women's Studies Program in conjunction with her counseling.

Ms. Manis has developed a number of workshops for women including ''Search,'' a workshop to help mature women reassess goals, ''Contact,'' to help separated and divorced women readjust to being alone, a ''Back-to-Work Clinic'' and ''A Woman's Place?'' for school age women to explore roles, plan ahead and learn some skills for more effective living. The text for *Womanpower* grew out of Ms. Manis' experiences in ''A Woman's Place?''

Prior to her work at Western Michigan University, Ms. Manis was Personnel Director at Doctors Hospital in New York City, Aptitude Test Evaluator for Johnson O'Connor Human Engineering Company and a high school counselor. She is author of two articles on women published in the *Personnel and Guidance Journal:* ''Search for Fulfillment,'' co-authored with June Mochizuki, and ''Disengagement in Women or How to Keep Marriage from being like Dying.''

Ms. Manis earned her Bachelor of Education in biology and social science at Chicago Teachers College and her Master of Arts in Counseling at Western Michigan University.

Library of Congress Cataloging in Publication Data

Manis, Laura G.
  Womanpower.
  Bibliography: p.
  1. Women — Psychology. 2. Group relations training. 3. College students — United States — Attitudes. 4. Self-actualization (Psychology).
  I. Title.
HQ1206.M34   158'.2   76-54156

Front cover design by the studio of Eurografica, Inc. Boston, Mass.

Illustrations selected from various sources of 19th century graphic art.

Manufactured in the United States of America

CONTENTS

CONTENTS

Preface

For a number of years I have worked in a program for adult, middle-aged women. The goal was to help these women gain better self-concepts enabling them to set meaningful goals for themselves. It became evident that a more useful expenditure of human potential would be to develop a program for much younger women of college or high school age. Such a program or workshop would help young women become aware of the problems they will face if they limit their planning to the first twenty years of their lives. They could be helped to avoid unsatisfactory stop-gap careers and to widen their horizons to more challenging and stimulating fields. At the same time, they could plan for the future so that the child-bearing years need not mean social isolation and a stoppage of participation with all the attendant fears, loss of self-esteem and guilt the older women had to resolve.

A colleague and I developed such a workshop aimed, hopefully, for a clientele of marriage-oriented students at the freshman-sophomore level. We called it ''A Woman's Place?'' After much publicity, the day of the first session arrived and twenty-three young women appeared. However, to our surprise, none of them were oriented toward the traditional marriage life-style. Our Workshop plans went out the window while we listened to these career-oriented young women tell us of their conflicts, anxieties, self-doubts and needs. Of course! Why hadn't this occurred to us? Women following a socially approved, traditional role have very few decisions to make. They think they know what's ahead and have no conflicts. Since they have none of these problems, why should they voluntarily attend a workshop of this sort? However, the women who did attend introduced us to an awareness of another population whose needs were not being met.

This manual was written in response to the needs of these women and also in response to the reports in the psychological literature concerning the ''new anxieties the current wave of feminism has unleashed.''[1] Rather than implying that feminism is harmful, it is more constructive to deal with the anxieties that social change — any social change — generates.

We are all aware of the enormous social changes that are presently occurring in our society. Major shifts in the roles of one of our largest ''minorities'' (in number) are one element in this social flux, and which few people can avoid dealing with at an

1. Moulton, Ruth, M.D., as quoted in *Behavior Today*, May 17, 1976.

v

intensely personal as well as abstract level. These changes have resulted from a movement aimed not only at increased access to society's resources and power, but also at a redefinition of who American women are and what they are worth. Such redefinition involves stress. It affects not only the women caught up in the process of change itself but also the men who are linked to it by the women with whom they have personal and working relationships and by its reciprocal effect on institutions, careers and lives.

Although this manual is directed mainly at career-oriented women, I have deliberately tried to balance the materials, both in tone and selection, to reach all women. Circumstances change — often without warning. A family-oriented woman may suddenly find herself compelled to support herself and a career woman may be required to spend some years entirely with her family. Moreover, it is my belief, that society will be better served when all persons, men and women, housewives and career women achieve self-actualization by having access to all options. Only then will having choices have real meaning.

Kalamazoo, Michigan   LAURA G. MANIS
November, 1976

Acknowledgements

I owe a debt of gratitude to over one-hundred young women and men who participated in the workshops that led to the development of this manual. They shared their problems, expressed their needs and, together, we enthusiastically and sometimes painfully searched out solutions. Their evaluations of the various experiences and exercises were a vital contribution.

A special word of thanks goes to colleagues Merry Pattison, Karen Little, and particularly to June Mochizuki, who served as group leaders and tested the exercises. Their perceptiveness and creativity stimulated and encouraged our approach.

My children, Bob and Lisa, have challenged me, each in their own way, from childhood to young adulthood. They have contributed much to my growth.

Finally, my husband Jerry Manis has been a model for person effectiveness. The management of his own life, the space he leaves for each of us to develop, his love and patience have been a constant source of support.

I. Introduction

Professionals in the educational and human services field know that more women are career-oriented than ever before, that more women are entering the labor force and that graduate school enrollments for women are increasing yearly.

However, a whole new set of problems have surfaced as a result of changing role expectations and women's growing freedom to aspire to new careers and higher achievement. In spite of their determination to have careers, these women are beset with conflicts, self-doubts and fears about their inadequacies. Roslyn S. Willett in "Working in a Man's World" (The Woman Executive by Gornick and Moran, 1971) states the problem succinctly:

> "This is a time of transition in the working
> relationships between women and men, character-
> ized by certain themes. One of them is women's
> poor image of themselves. Believing themselves
> to be lesser, smaller, weaker, more passive,
> more trivial, incapable of taking hold of a big job,
> they behave as if they are this way and then get
> confirmation from others in their own beliefs."

In addition, Matina Horner (1970, 1972) has well documented the fear women have of success which inhibits the normal motivation for achievement most bright women have. Mental health workers know, moreover, that changing or changed perceptions of self and society generate new sources of conflict, ambivalence, guilt and shame, as well as new sources and patterns of aspiration (Westervelt, 1973).

*Rosylyn S. Willett, "Working in 'A Man's World'" in *Women in Sexist Society* ed. by Vivian Gornick and Barbara Moran (New York: Signet Books, 1972), p. 512.

That so many career-oriented women have problems is to be expected. Our culture produces women who are largely passive, dependent and indecisive. This is the norm and everyone (parents, teachers, mental health workers and the women themselves) expects and values this behavior. Women exhibiting contrary behavior are looked upon as maladjusted even by therapists (Broverman, et. al., 1970). As a result, most women are deficient in the very behaviors necessary to succeed in a career, or for that matter, to feel adequate or to become self-actualizing.

Bardwick and Douvan (1971) contend that the tragedy for some women is their desire to succeed in competitive achievement while they hold in contempt the traditional role for which they are better equipped.

In point of fact, however, it is negligent for human services professionals, parents and teachers not to prepare women students to achieve successfully in order to be ready for what is almost certain to be ahead for them. The necessity for this action is shown by the Department of Labor statistics (1973) stating that nine out of ten women work sometime in their lives and two-thirds of the women are in the work force because of economic necessity. They are paid less and are at the bottom in all fields. One-third of all working women were in seven occupations in the late 1960's.

Therefore, it is the responsibility of professionals to equip women to succeed competitively in the world of work. This manual was developed as a tool to be used in fulfilling this responsibility.

Population

The materials for this manual were developed as a result of two years' experience working with approximately 129 college students, 117 women and 12 men in nine experimental groups originally called "A Woman's Place?" They demonstrated that there is a population eager for an opportunity to equip themselves better for the future. Their needs, responses and evaluations provide the basis for the structure and content of this program.

While a few men attended some of the workshops, the majority contained only women. Whether or not men should be included can be left up to the leader and participants. Experience has shown that both types of groups showed growth in different ways. The mixed groups exacerbated certain problem areas, such as women deferring to the men's opinions, feeling inhibited, showing dependence and retreating into a sheltered environment. The emotions and behaviors exhibited there most approximated real life. The single-sexed groups were more supportive and the participants were able to clarify their feelings, to "get their heads together." When asked why they joined, the women made such statements as —

"I'm just tired of being meek, labeled and used; I want to see if I can change."

"I'd like to change or determine my feelings of being an assistant when I would prefer to be a leader."

"I don't know the real role of a woman, especially in a career."

"I need more self-confidence and pride in being a female. It's a constant struggle to decide about my future."

The men, on the other hand, stated that they joined to find out what women are really concerned about and to exchange ideas. They felt they could talk more honestly in a workshop like this where there were no social or sexual expectations.

The difference in motivation for joining and the difference in sex ratio could, however, be the result of the publicity. A workshop billed as a program for developing personal effectiveness will draw a clientele of males and females quite different from a program billed as one exploring women's roles.

In any case, each exercise or strategy in the manual is suitable or can be easily adapted for either mixed-sex groups or women-only groups. The materials selected are meant to be used for high school and college age students and young adults. While the activities in this manual are discussed in the context of a small group setting, many can be used in the classroom or with individuals. Classes concerning women in social science, sociology, history, management psychology, and status of women are especially suitable.

Goals

The behavior traits thought most characteristic of "healthy" adults, as described in Broverman (1970), and of those adults thought most capable of fulfilling their greatest potential or being "self-actualizing" are usually considered to be —

>Independence
>Decisiveness
>Active, rather than passive, behavior
>Assertiveness
>Openness
>Self-confidence and willingness to risk.

Other components of behavior necessary to achieve the above are —

>Self-awareness
>Values clarification
>Communication and feedback
>Improved interpersonal relationships

As it developed during discussions of the participants' motives for joining the experimental program, these were the traits they felt they most needed to develop and strengthen.

Accordingly, the goals listed in the description of the planning sessions were developed by the participants of the first experimental workshops. They describe the needs expressed by the participants plus the behavior traits previously mentioned.

Current workshops should begin with a discussion of the individual needs of the persons present and whether or not the goals listed fit each person. Participants may modify or suggest other goals either for themselves or for the entire group.

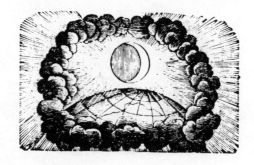

Procedure

Since one of the goals of the program is to produce active, effective, assertive and decisive women, the participants are actively involved in the planning and evaluating of each session. The planning session is devoted to —

1. Getting to know one another and each one's aspirations and needs;

2. Discussing the goals of the individual participants of the workshop;

3. Planning for the next sessions.

This manual will include a detailed description of the planning session only. Each of the following sessions are developed by both leader and participants. Together they will select materials from the manual that fit the priorities and needs of the group. (See "How To Use This Manual.")

Evaluation and Planning

An important part of the program is the time set aside at the end of every session to evaluate the day's proceedings, and to solicit suggestions. This time is also used periodically to assess whether or not the priorities decided upon during the first session still fit or whether they need to be modified. Consideration should be given to such questions as —

Are more sessions needed for the particular skill we are working on?

Would the next priority be more effective before or after learning another skill?

During the first sessions or until the participants feel comfortable and assertive enough to evaluate without structure, the participants can be asked to complete orally the exercise on evaluation taken from Simon, et. al. (1972). This exercise is described in the detailed explanation of the planning session.

We have found that participants are encouraged to respond, feel more accepted and gain more experience in risking if the leader listens and allows the participants to make critical evaluations without responding defensively. Of course, the leader must show that the workshop will respond to the suggestions in later sessions. The leader can ask questions for clarification. Other participants may be asked for their reactions to another participant's evaluations.

How To Use This Manual

Except for the planning session, each of the other sessions are planned and structured by the participants. For this reason, the manual is divided into sections by topics. A list of eight topics and a brief description of the strategies for implementing them is included in the planning session. The group and leader can select the exercises or strategies that best fit them, can select as many or as few as they think necessary to fully explore or develop a behavior skill and can spend as many sessions as necessary on each topic.

All activities in the manual have been selected because of their appropriateness to women's needs in relation to goals of the program. In addition, where necessary, they have been designed or modified to deal with behaviors from a woman's perspective.

Some of the activities in this book have not appeared previously in print. Several of them have been suggested by other leaders or by participants and it has usually been difficult, if not impossible, to identify the original source. Wherever an activity has come to us from an identifiable source, we have tried our best to give appropriate credit.

Generally, each activity is described in a standard format for experiencing, learning and practicing the planned skills. In some sections, some information is provided or a concept is explained. The format is as follows:

1. Purpose — how it relates to one or more of the eight topics.

2. Mini-discussion — a brief warm-up discussion which permits participants to recall previous experiences and reactions as they relate to the activity.

3. Procedures — a detailed description including approximate time involved, materials needed, and steps to follow.

4. Discussion — suggestions for leading discussion in order to integrate and assess learning, explore meaning and effect.

5. Notes and suggestions to the leader — and additional variations or uses when appropriate.

6. References or bibliography — where necessary

This format has been used for the sake of clarity only. There is no one right way to carry out these activities. Change them. Think of your own. Use your own examples.

Although the original experimental workshops consisted of six two-hour sessions, a program can be planned to fit any structure from a classroom situation meeting for an entire semester, one hour each session, to a workshop setting of six, eight or more sessions, two hours in length. The teacher or leader, with the help of the participants, will have to determine how much time to spend on each activity and on the discussions before and after an activity. The approximate time for each activity is included in the description. However, it is much better to explore each topic to its fullest than to keep to a rigid time schedule.

Role of the Leader

In a program attempting to develop leadership and assertiveness, it is best that the leader participates as a member of the group. The leader does the activities, shares her reactions and contributes her own experiences. She serves as a model demonstrating how to be open, willing to risk, and a good listener. She shows by her verbal and non-verbal communication that she is interested in what the participants think and will seriously consider their suggestions and possibly be influenced by them. This encourages an atmosphere of openness, honesty, acceptance and respect. If the participants feel that something they say about their own behavior or beliefs is going to be ridiculed by the other group members or not accepted by the leader, they will not want to share their thoughts and feelings.

When an exercise calls for an expression of feelings, or any other risk taking, the leader can respond first. This establishes a model for the behavior expected and clarifies the procedure for the activity. However, when opinions are solicited or decisions are to be made, the best time for the leader to give her view (in order not to influence decisions) is toward the end after the other members of the group have had a chance to think things through for themselves and express their own views.

The leader is also a person with many of the same problems facing the members, some resolved and some unresolved. She should present herself that way. Most important is demonstrating that there is no one solution or behavior style that fits everyone. Each person must work out the style that best suits her. Everyone's contributions are of equal value. The particular content of the leader's choices hold no more weight than anyone else's. However, her behavior can strengthen the process of growing.

We wish you success in the use of any of these activities and would welcome any ideas, adaptations or suggestions. Please send your contribution to the author or to the Counseling Center, Western Michigan University, Kalamazoo, Michigan 49008. If any materials are used in any further publications, they will be gratefully acknowledged.

References

1. Bardwick & Douvan, E. "Ambivalence: The Socialization of Women." In Gornick & Moran (Eds.) *Women in a Sexist Society*. New York: Basic Books, Inc., 1971, 147-154.
2. Broverman, I. K., Broverman, D. M., Clarkson, F. E., Rosenkrantz, P. S., & Vogel, S. R. "Sex-role Stereotypes and Clinical Judgments of Mental Health." *Journal of Consulting and Clinical Psychology*, 1970, *34*, 1-7.
3. Gardner, JoAnn, "Sexist Counseling Must Stop." *Personnel and Guidance Journal*, Vol. 49, No. 9, May, 1971. pp. 705-712.
4. Horner, Matina S. "Femininity and Successful Achievement: A Basic Inconsistency." Chapter 3 in *Feminine Personality and Conflict* ed. by J. M. Bardwick, E. Douvan, M. S. Horner, & D. Gutman (Eds.). E. L. Walker, Belmont, Cal.: Brooks/Cole, 1970.
5. Horner, M. S. "Toward an Understanding of Achievement-Related Conflicts in Women. *Journal of Social Issues*, 1972, Vol. *28*, pp. 157-175.
6. Simon, S. B., Howe, L. W., & Kirschenbaum, *Values Clarification: A Handbook of Practical Strategies for Teachers and Students*. New York: Hart Publishing Co., 1972.
7. U.S. Department of Labor. *Facts About Women Workers*. Washington, D.C.: Women's Bureau, No. 358-11704, 1972.
8. Westervelt, E. "A Tide in the Affairs of Women: The Psychological Impact of Feminism on Educated Women." *The Counseling Psychologist*, 1973, Vol. *4*, pp. 3-25.
9. Willett, Roslyn S., "Working in a Man's World: The Woman Executive" Chapter 22, in *Women in a Sexist Society*, edited by Gornick and Moran. New York: Basic Books, Inc., 1971. pp. 511-522.

II. Planning Session

Getting started: Some facts we all should know, learning about the workshop, setting goals, and setting priorities.

"Anything may happen when womanhood has ceased to be a protected occupation . . . ."

Virginia Woolf

exercise one: *15 minutes*

1   *Do You Know?*

Purpose: To acquaint you with some facts you need to know
so that you can prepare yourself for the future.

Looking Ahead

Before we start, it is important to know some facts
about women and society. If you are going to make plans
and prepare yourselves for the future, you will be interested in the following information.

Procedure: Please read —

The twentieth century has brought about one of the most
dramatic changes for women by lengthening their life spans from
less than 50 years to over 75 years.

1900 — 48 years

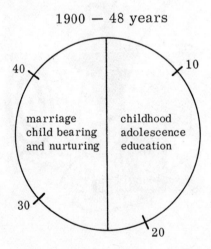

Marriage later in life, most had
children and large families. Not
many years of active life after
last child raised.

1970 — 75 years

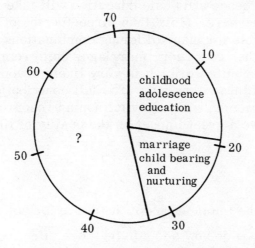

Earlier marriage and earlier
completion of families alter
the life pattern greatly. Most
women continue to marry and
have children. Now half their
lives are before them after the
most time-consuming child
rearing years are over.

It is predicted that by the year 2000, women will live
up to 100 years of age

100 years in year 2000

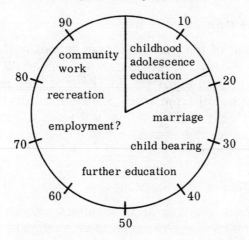

Childhood, adolescence and basic education will take less than
a quarter of those years. More than three-fourths of a woman's
life will be available for many differing combinations of —
employment, further education, marriage, child rearing, re-
creation and community work. It is very likely a woman's life
will contain all of these elements. The full contribution of
citizens who are women will be a vital human resource in the
year 2000 and have a great impact on the quality of life for the
entire society. *

Discussion:

What are the implications of the above for you as a woman?

What can you do now so as to be more effective in the future?

———

*From *Women, Report of the National Advisory Commission on the Status of Women*. State of California,
Document Section, 1971. Leaflet.

Career Expectations

5 minutes

We're sure you will be interested in reading the following.
Looking ahead to the next 20 or 30 years doesn't require a crystal
ball. According to the Department of Labor Statistics* the chances
are that you will —

Work some time in your life

Nine out of ten women now in school will be employed
in the future. Most women will spend 25 years or
more at paid employment, even if they marry and
take time off from work to raise children. In 1973,
45 per cent of all American women worked and 42.9
per cent of these women had children under 18
years of age.

Work because of economic need

Nearly two-thirds of all women workers are single,
divorced or separated or have husbands who earn
between $7,000 and $9,999 per year.

———

*U.S. Department of Labor, Women's Bureau, *Highlights of Women's Employment and Education*, rev. ed.
Washington, D.C., Supt. of Documents. June, 1974.

UNLESS you start preparing NOW, you will —

Be at the bottom of your field

The proportion of professional and technical workers
who are women decreased. In 1930, 44. 8 per cent
of all professional and technical workers were women.
In 1972 this proportion had decreased to 39. 3 per cent.

Be paid less than men doing equal work

Starting salaries are lower for women than for men.
The median annual earnings for year-round full-time
women workers is 57 per cent of men's.

Be in only one of seven job areas

The large majority of women are still in teaching,
nursing, social work, librarianship, sales, clerical
and service occupations.

How can you prepare NOW to be more EFFECTIVE in the FUTURE?

exercise two: *15 minutes*

2   *Setting Goals*

Purpose: To agree on individual and group goals.

Discussion:

A good way to get started is to get to know one another and why we are here. Let's go around the circle and briefly give our names, a sentence or two about who we are, why we joined and what we expect to be doing in five years.

Procedure:

Below are goals participants in previous workshops decided they would like to work toward. Please read them and think about your own reasons for joining.

Goals for this Workshop:

1. To increase the participants' understanding of the forces in our society and the forces within themselves that can limit their choices in personal and vocational decisions.

2. To teach the participants how they may control and expand their choices and behavior and not be thus limited in their alternatives.

3. To develop or strengthen the abilities of the participants to communicate, to be assertive, to evaluate, to clarify values and to make independent decisions using these skills as tools to design a life style that fits them.

4. To give emotional support to those women who are experiencing pressures from society and peers because their decisions are different from the average.

Discussion:

Do these goals fit you and other members of the group? Are there any others you would like to suggest?

exercise three: *10 minutes*

Techniques Used 3

Purpose: To understand the techniques of group effort in achieving personal goals.

Workshops by their very nature provide the opportunity for personal interaction among the participants. We will work together to develop our awareness and understanding and to learn new skill-building techniques. Sharing common problems, exchanging ideas, defining objectives and participating in small group experiences using the following techniques are all part of this workshop.

Procedure: Please read —

A variety of techniques will be employed. They are:

1. Exercises — which lead us to experience the relevant concepts and to practice applying these concepts.

2. Discussions — which will provide for the exchange of ideas and clarification of concepts.

3. Outside activities — which will involve us in doing something outside the classroom on a more practical level.

4. Role-play — which provides a vicarious experience, a change of pace and an opportunity for added involvement.

5. Simulation — which provides miniature models of the environment in which we may actually be living sometime in the future. Participating in a simulation gives us practice in a more lifelike situation and provides another avenue for experience.

Discussion:

If you have any questions or concerns about the above techniques, ask your leader to clarify them for you.

exercise four: *45 minutes*

4   *What's Your Space?*

Purpose: To help you understand your own behavior patterns
and set some personal goals.

Let's start from where you are. How do you feel
about men? women? adults? yourself? Where do
these feelings come from? What part has your family?
church? school? society? played in the development of
these feelings?

On the following page is a simple exercise designed
to help you sort out these feelings and clarify their
origins. It will also help you set some personal goals
and make plans for other sessions of the workshop.
The exercise has three parts. Your leader will describe
each part separately.

Procedure: Part 1

(A)   Your leader will divide the group into three sections.
         Each section is assigned a category — either "men",
         "women", or "adult". Write your assigned title in the
         blank space _____ Category on the
         Behavior Traits Chart on the following page.

(B)   The phrases along the sides of the page are the extremes
         of each behavior trait. The boxes in between the phrases
         mark the distance or closeness to each extreme. The
         middle figure, No. 4, is neutral.

(C)   Place an X under the number which you believe best
         describes persons in general in the category assigned
         to you. Try to avoid using No. 4.

Behavior Traits Chart

Category

	1	2	3	4	5	6	7	
Not at all courageous								Very courageous
Not at all independent								Very independent
Shows emotions								Never shows emotions
Very subjective								Very objective
Very easily influenced								Not at all easily influenced
Very submissive								Very dominant
Very passive								Very active
Not at all competitive								Very competitive
Very indirect								Very direct
Has difficulty making decisions								Can make decisions easily
Not at all confident								Very self-confident
Not very ambitious								Very ambitious
Very uncomfortable about being aggressive								Not all uncomfortable about being aggressive

Directions:

1. Place an X under the number which you believe best describes persons in general in the category assigned to you. (Wait for instructions from leader before continuing.)

2. Place an "M" closest to the poles which best describe you.

3. Place a "G" in the box which indicates where you would like to be.

Discussion:

This is a replication of a research done by Broverman et al. * with 77 mental health workers. Are most women toward the left pole? Are most men and adults toward the right pole? (The results of the Broverman research were similar to yours.)

How would you expect a woman to be treated by her family and friends if she doesn't fit what society sees as the "normal" or "average" characteristics for a woman?

If she goes for help to a teacher or mental health worker, how would she be treated?

How does she feel about being different?

What does it mean that the behavior expected for men and adults are similar but for women are different?

How do the expectations of our society about men and women affect their behavior and feelings about themselves?

Part 2

In order for you to see how our culture has affected you personally, rate yourself on the same Chart using an "M" for me in the boxes closest to the poles which best describe you.

Part 3

Are you dissatisfied with how you see yourself in any of these behaviors?

Would you like to change or move in another direction on any of the traits?

When you think about your future or your career, will you have to learn new behaviors or strengthen some others?

Place a "G" (goal) in the box which best indicates where you would like to be.

Discussion:

Share with the other members of the group one of the behaviors you would like to change.

*I. K. Broverman et al., "Sex Role Stereotypes and Clinical Judgments of Mental Health," in *Journal of Consulting and Clinical Psychology*. Vol. 34, 1970. p. 1-7.

To the Leader:

> Point out to the group any common areas of concern, common goals. Are there certain traits which most of the participants have in common, certain traits many would like to change?

exercise five: *30 minutes*

Checklist for Planning Future Sessions   **5**

Purpose: To establish the direction and structure for future sessions.

> During the next few weeks we will be working on the traits we would most like to change and trying to resolve or clarify the issues of most concern to us.

Procedure:

> Below is a list of topics suggested by other groups which have been most effective. Think about your own needs and the goals of the workshop while you read over the list. Your leader will answer any questions you may have about any of the items and give you some examples of the various strategies. Do you have any others of special interest you would like to add? List them in the blank spaces and bring them up during the general discussion of the topics. Other members may be concerned about them also but may not have thought of them.

Individual Decision	Topics	Group Decision
_____	1. Assertiveness Training: Practice in increasing degrees of self-assertion using role playing in real life situations; how to handle "put downs", how to say "no" and express needs.	_____
_____	2. Decision Making: Using values, setting priorities, overcoming barriers.	_____
_____	3. Improving Communication in Interpersonal Relationships: Using listening and feedback techniques; conflict resolution; expressing feelings constructively.	_____

Individual Decision	Topics	Group Decision
_____	4. Leadership Training: Learning skills of empathic listening, group techniques, discussion leading and decision making.	_____
_____	5. Men-Women Relationships: Discussion and role playing of problem areas, life styles and roles.	_____
_____	6. Planning for Contingencies of the Future: A simulation in which you describe your future plans and then try to answer questions from the others; such as — "What will you do if . . . ?" Foreseeing and planning for times of conflict and pressure.	_____
_____	7. Role Models: Inviting successful career women to a session to talk about their careers, their peak decisions, their problems, enlarging options, learning about other women's life styles.	_____
_____	8. Values Clarification: Finding out what's important to you, a necessary component for making satisfactory decisions.	_____
_____	9. Other: _____	_____

Now that you have read over the suggested topics and understand what may be involved in each topic, write your ranking preference in the left hand column, checking as No. 1 the topic you consider most important and so on down to the least important for you as No. 8 or 9. Do not discuss your ranking with others in the group.

Then, as a group, try to reach consensus as to the rank order of all the items. Write the group decision in the right hand column.

To the Leader:

If the leader wishes, this may be used as an exercise in group dynamics following the procedures in "What's My Behavior in a Task Group" on page 118. However, at this stage, all feedback should be positive and the group may be too new for such an experiment.

exercise six: *15 minutes*

Evaluation

6

Purpose: To practice evaluating what you learn at each session.

At the end of every session you will be asked to evaluate that day's proceedings and will be asked for any suggestions. Since each workshop is different because of the differing needs of the participants, your leader(s) will be constantly consulting with you to check your reactions to use as a guide for future sessions.

Procedure: At the beginning, you may find using the following phrases helpful. Learning to use such phrases is helpful in expressing reactions and needs in work, family, and classroom situations. Pick one phrase or a combination of phrases to complete which best summarize your reaction to that day's proceedings. Share the phrases with your group. *

I learned . . .	or I wonder if . . .
I realized . . .	I wonder why . . .
I was surprised . . .	I wonder how . . .
I was pleased . . .	I wonder when . . .
I was displeased . . .	I wonder about . . .

To the Leader:

After the first evaluation session, repeat for emphasis the usefulness of the above phrases in other situations. We also will be using the "I" statements to give us practice in taking responsibility for our own statements, opinions, and feelings.

------

*From Sidney B. Simon, Leland W. Howe and Howard Kirschenbaum, *Values Clarification*. (New York: Hart Publishing Co., 1972) pp. 163, 166.

exercise seven: *30 minutes*

7   *Organization of Support Groups*

                        (For Leaders)

Purpose: To work out a pattern for setting up sub-groups.

Many of the strategies and exercises suggested in
this manual call for breaking up the workshop into small
groupings. It is much easier and takes a shorter time
to build a trusting atmosphere in a small group. Each
member competes less for "air time."

Procedure and Discussion:

The leader explains to group that they will be working
in small groups occasionally. She explains that it is better
not to work with old friends but rather to try to build a
listening, trusting climate with other people as well.

1. Persons move around and greet each other
    non-verbally. At the end of a few minutes,
    each person selects someone she would
    like to know better.

2. Each pair spends five minutes getting to
    know each other.

3. Pairs move around for a few minutes.

4. Each pair picks another pair they would like
    to be with and spends five minutes getting
    acquainted.

5. Repeat process until groups of six or eight,
    or whatever number leader has decided upon,
    are reached.

The same support group can be used whenever an
activity calls for a small grouping. If an activity calls
for a diad, the small group breaks up into its original
pairs. However, avoid over-using support groups. It
is important that students work with persons from all
groups and have opportunities to apply their learnings
to other group situations. Therefore, when an exercise
needs small groupings, sometimes the leader may ask
the workshop to break into support groups and, at other
times new groupings can be formed.

III. Values Clarification

Finding out what's important to you; a necessary component for making satisfactory decisions. Where do you learn your values? How do you use them?

Things I Like to Do
What Would You Do?
Forced Choice Value Inventory
Values Bidding

"This is a confusing world to live in. At every turn we are forced to make choices about how to live our lives. Ideally, our choices will be made on the basis of the values we hold; but frequently, we are not clear about our own values."
Sidney G. Simon, Leland W. Howe, Howard Kirschenbaum, *(Values Clarification, N.Y. Hart, 1972)*

exercise eight: *45 minutes*

8   *Things I Like To Do*

Purpose: To help you learn the origins and relative importance of some of your values.

We make decisions based on what is important to us. What is important can be called our values. We learn our values from our parents, church, school, friends and our culture. They change according to our circumstances in life, our age, conflicts with other values, people who are important, and priorities of needs.

Valuing, then, is a process which is used whenever choices are to be made. Because people state that they value something does not necessarily mean they do; for example, people who espouse ecology but litter roads and parks. Valuing, according to Raths (1966), is composed of seven sub-processes.*

1. Prizing and cherishing one's belief and behaviors

2. Publicly affirming, when appropriate

3. Choosing from alternatives

4. Choosing after consideration of consequences

5. Choosing freely

6. Acting on one's beliefs

7. Acting with a pattern, consistency and repetition."

The following exercise will initiate a realization of certain values, their origins and relative importance.

------

*Louis S. Raths, Merril Harmin and Sidney Simon, *Values and Teaching*. (Columbus, Ohio: Charles E. Merrill Co., 1966) p. 30.

Discussion: When you get out of bed in the morning, what is the first decision you must make? What values are you using? On some mornings do you make a decision that is different from usual? What has happened to the original values? Where did you learn these values? The next exercise will make you aware of other values you hold and, possibly, where you learned them.

Procedure:

1.   List in the first column of the chart on the next page fifteen things that you enjoy doing. Work quickly; write down the first things that come to your mind. List things that make you happy, are fun, that you enjoy and that make you feel good. There are no right or wrong answers about what you should like.

2.   Fill in the other columns according to the following directions:

$3.00   Place a $ sign by any activity that costs more than $3.00 each time you do it.

Alone/   Put an "A" for activities which you prefer
People   doing alone; a "P" for those you prefer doing with people.

Risk   Put an "R" by each activity you would be willing to declare in public.

3 yr.   Check those you would have listed three years ago.

M/F   Using the letters "M" and "F", record which activities you think your mother and father would also list.

Last   Write the approximate date you last did
Date   this activity.

Times   How many times this year did you do it? Write "N" for never, "S" for seldom, "F" for frequently, and "VF" for very frequently.

U   Place the letter "U" next to the activity that you think others would consider unconventional.

Rank   Number 1 through 5 the activities you like to do best.

Things I Like To Do *

15 Things I Like To Do	$3	Alone/ People	Risk	3 yr.	M/F	U	Times	Last Date	Rank
1.									
2.									
3.									
4.									
5.									
6.									
7.									
8.									
9.									
10.									
11.									
12.									
13.									
14.									
15.									

Discussion:

Review your lists. What did you learn about yourself? How would an explorer from another planet describe your values? Are there some things you like to do that you have not done lately? Are your values more like your mother's or your father's?

———

*Modified from H. B. Gelatt, Barbara Varenhorst and Richard Carey, *Deciding*. (New York: College Entrance Examination Board, 1972) p. 28.

exercise nine: *60 minutes*

What Would You Do?   **9**

Purpose: To expose you to a variety of possible decisions based
on different value emphases.

It is important to understand that other people's
values may be different from yours and to be tolerant.
Values are neither right or wrong. Different values are
important to different people. This exercise demonstrates
that holding different values leads people to make different
decisions. Even though the decisions are different, they
are equally satisfying if they meet the values of the people
who have them.

Discussion: Think of a decision you reached today (what to
wear, what to eat, whether to eat). What decision did
the others in your group reach about the same item?
Why did they reach different decisions?

Procedure:

1.   Listed below are some values many people have.
      There are many others, probably some which you
      feel are more important.

family relations	recognition and prestige
responsibility	education
pleasure	creativity
wealth	approval of others
independence	helping others

Read the stories that follow. If you were the person
in the story, what would you decide under the circumstances?

2.   From the list of values above, choose the values
      you think the decision represents. If there is none
      that you think fits, write your idea of the value or
      values.

KATHY

Kathy is very active and dedicated to the woman's movement. She also enjoys doing things with her hands and fixing things. She feels very strongly that women should be self-reliant and able to take care of themselves in an emergency. Next year her high school is starting a new course in auto mechanics — open, of course, to both male and female students. She has one elective not committed to subjects she absolutely has to take. However, she wants to go to the state university, which suggests that she take another year of a foreign language. What course should Kathy take for the elective?

Kathy decides to ....

She values ....

MS. BRIGHTON

Ms. Brighton, a single parent, is a design director at Creative Enterprises, Inc. She is making $15,000 a year, enjoying the chance to draw, use her creative ideas and see some of them developed. Her oldest daughter will be entering college next September which will be a drain on the family finances. There are three other children in the family. She is also beginning to worry about how to manage replacing some worn-out major appliances. She is called into the president's office and offered the job of assistant vice president at a salary of $22,000 a year. She would be handling production, personnel problems and sales. There would not be time for creative work and the parts of her job she enjoys.

Ms. Brighton decides to ....

She values ....

DEBBIE

Debbie and Bob marry in the spring of her junior year. Bob is a senior. Both have scholarships and Bob plans for a fellowship to graduate school. The future looks like clear sailing and Debbie has promised her father to continue school until she gets her bachelor's degree. He will pay for her tuition and living expenses as he had before the marriage. Then the blow falls — Bob does not get his fellowship but graduate work is essential in his field of engineering.

Debbie decides to ....

She values ....

LISA

Lisa is interested in music and has studied the flute for the past five years. She also loves children — taking care of them, teaching them, playing with them. In June she is invited to join the community civic orchestra for the summer. She would be paid $2.50 an hour. At the same time she is asked to be a camp leader working with visually handicapped children. She would be paid $2.50 an hour for the camp job, too. She is not able to accept both invitations.

Lisa decides to ....

She values ....

Discussion: Discuss the different decisions members of your group have reached and the different values each has chosen. Which decisions are "better"? How are values used in making decisions?

exercise ten: *60 minutes*

10   *Forced Choice Value Inventory*

Purpose: To confront the stresses involved in setting priorities
for your values.

      It can be very helpful in decision-making and setting
goals if we can identify our values. However, many
decisions may require having to choose between two or
more important values. Making a decision is not simple.
Not only may we have to give up a value we believe is
important in favor of a higher priority one, we may have
to defend our decisions to persons with different value
systems. The following exercise forces a choice among
values. By so doing you can arrive at a ranking of your
values.

Discussion: Can you think of a situation where you had to
make a decision when two or more values conflicted?
(Example: education or good grades vs. loyalty to
friends)

Procedure:

    1.   Look over the list of values and their definitions on
the following pages. These are values many people
feel are important. Of course, there are many others
we were not able to include here. Define the values
according to definitions listed so that everyone in
your group is using words in the same way.

    2.   Do the Forced Choice Value Inventory on the pages
following the definitions.

Definitions of Selected Values

AESTHETICS — Appreciation and enjoyment of beauty for
beauty's sake

AMBITION — Strong desire for achievement

APPEARANCE — Concern for the attractiveness of one's
own person

BROAD-MINDEDNESS — Open-minded, tolerant

COMPETENCE — Capable, effective

CREATIVITY — Imaginative

EMOTIONAL HEALTH — Peace of mind, freedom from
overwhelming anxiety

EQUALITY — Equal opportunity for all

ETHICS — Having principles of conduct

HELPFULNESS — Working for or devotion to others

HONESTY — Truthful, sincere

KNOWLEDGE — Seeking of truth, information

LEADERSHIP — Influence over others

LEISURE — Time for enjoyment, gratification

LOVE — Devotion, warm attachment that prizes another

PHYSICAL HEALTH — Freedom from physical disease
or pain

POPULARITY — Being liked, approved and accepted
by many

RELIGIOUS FAITH — Obedience to and activity in behalf
of a Supreme Being

SECURITY — Freedom from concern for material resources

SELF-SUFFICIENCY — Self-reliant, independent

SUCCESS — Accomplishment brought about by effort and
determination

Forced Choice Value Inventory

Directions: Each item contains a group of characteristics. In each grouping you are to rate the value you place on each characteristic. There are no right or wrong answers. Rate the values according to how you really feel, not how you should feel. In front of each characteristic you are to place a number from 1 (the characteristic you value most in the grouping) to 5 (the characteristic you value the least). Be sure you place a number from 1 to 5 in front of each characteristic. You must give a different rating to each characteristic named in the group.

1. ____ Ambition
   ____ Broadmindedness
   ____ Competence
   ____ Popularity
   ____ Helpfulness

2. ____ Broadmindedness
   ____ Creativity
   ____ Self-Sufficiency
   ____ Physical Health
   ____ Aesthetics

3. ____ Creativity
   ____ Security
   ____ Popularity
   ____ Appearance
   ____ Love

4. ____ Security
   ____ Success
   ____ Leadership
   ____ Ambition
   ____ Physical Health

5. ____ Success
   ____ Honesty
   ____ Appearance
   ____ Knowledge
   ____ Broadmindedness

6. ____ Honesty
   ____ Competence
   ____ Creativity
   ____ Leadership
   ____ Leisure

7. ____ Competence
   ____ Self-Suficiency
   ____ Knowledge
   ____ Emotional Health
   ____ Security

8. ____ Self-Sufficiency
   ____ Popularity
   ____ Leisure
   ____ Religious Faith
   ____ Success

9. ____ Popularity
   ____ Physical Health
   ____ Emotional Health
   ____ Equality
   ____ Honesty

10. ____ Physical Health
    ____ Appearance
    ____ Religious Faith
    ____ Ethics
    ____ Competent

11. ____ Appearance
    ____ Leadership
    ____ Helpfulness
    ____ Self-Sufficiency
    ____ Equality

12. ____ Leadership
    ____ Knowledge
    ____ Ethics
    ____ Aesthetics
    ____ Popularity

13. ____ Knowledge
    ____ Leisure
    ____ Physical Health
    ____ Helpfulness
    ____ Love

14. ____ Leisure
    ____ Emotional Health
    ____ Aesthetics
    ____ Ambition
    ____ Appearance

15. ____ Emotional Health
    ____ Religious Faith
    ____ Love
    ____ Broadmindedness
    ____ Leadership

16. ____ Religious Faith
    ____ Equality
    ____ Ambition
    ____ Creativity
    ____ Knowledge

17. ____ Equality
    ____ Ethics
    ____ Broadmindedness
    ____ Security
    ____ Leisure

18. ____ Ethics
    ____ Helpfulness
    ____ Success
    ____ Emotional Health
    ____ Creativity

19. ____ Helpfulness
    ____ Aesthetics
    ____ Security
    ____ Honesty
    ____ Religious Faith

20. ____ Aesthetics
    ____ Love
    ____ Equality
    ____ Success
    ____ Competence

21. ____ Love
    ____ Ambition
    ____ Honesty
    ____ Self-Sufficiency
    ____ Ethics

Scoring

Directions for Scoring: Each value appeared in different groupings five times on the preceding page. After each value on the scoring chart below, place the numbers you assigned to it each time that value appeared. Then add the total numbers across.

Below the tabulating chart, list the values starting with the lowest totals and so on for all 21 values. This list will show the values of most importance to you.

Tabulating Sheet — Value Inventory

VALUE	Number of group listing this value	Your ratings for each time value appeared					Total
		1	2	3	4	5	
Aesthetics	2, 12, 14, 19, 20						
Ambition	1, 4, 14, 16, 21						
Appearance	3, 5, 10, 11, 14						
Broadmindedness	1, 2, 5, 15, 17						
Competence	1, 6, 7, 10, 20						
Creativity	2, 3, 6, 16, 18						
Emotional Health	7, 9, 14, 15, 18						
Equality	9, 11, 16, 17, 20						
Ethics	10, 12, 17, 18, 21						
Helpfulness	1, 11, 13, 18, 19						
Honesty	5, 6, 9, 19, 21						
Knowledge	5, 7, 12, 13, 16						
Leadership	4, 6, 11, 12, 15						
Leisure	6, 8, 13, 14, 17						
Love	3, 13, 15, 20, 21						
Physical Health	2, 4, 9, 10, 13						
Popularity	1, 3, 8, 9, 12						
Religious Faith	8, 10, 15, 16, 19						
Security	3, 4, 7, 17, 19						
Self-Sufficiency	2, 7, 8, 11, 21						
Success	4, 5, 8, 18, 20						

Values in Order of Importance

1. ....
2. ....
3. ....
4. ....
5. ....
6. ....
7. ....

8. ....
9. ....
10. ....
11. ....
12. ....
13. ....
14. ....

15. ....
16. ....
17. ....
18. ....
19. ....
20. ....
21. ....

Discussion: (In support groups of six)

We have found in discussions with other groups
that usually the first five values are goals we are working
to obtain. The next ten or so are still important to us
but they may already be part of our lives and taken for
granted. The last few are values we reject.

Discuss whether this describes your rankings.
Were there any surprises? If there are any, do they
fit you? Is this the way you really feel or did you give
higher or lower rankings according to what your current
peer group values or rejects rather than your true feelings?

To the Leader:

On page 119 you will find an exercise which can be
used here if your group wishes to include it. The
exercise called "How Well Are Our Institutions
Serving The Country?" involves societal values and
the participants' willingness to defend their values
publicly.

exercise eleven: *60 minutes*

11   *Values Bidding*

Purpose: To test your self-understanding regarding your
personal values code.

The Values Bidding adds another dimension to the
assessment of values — that of emotion. It is one thing
to decide intellectually what we value; it is quite another
to find out what we would really fight for. When emotions
are involved, we sometimes become aware of other values
we did not realize were so important.

Discussion: If participants have already done the Values
Inventory, ask them to note their five top values on a
separate sheet of paper. If they have not, ask all
persons to list what they believe to be their top five values.

---

*Idea from James McHolland, *Value Auction Exercise of Human Potential Seminars* (Evanston, Illinois:
unpublished leaflet).

Procedure:

1. Look at the Values Bidding Tally Sheet. Each of these items will be auctioned off to the highest bidder. You have $4,000 to use. Take five minutes to budget this amount among the items on the sheet. You can spend your money on one, two or three items or on as many as you wish so long as you <u>do not exceed your total budget of $4,000</u>.

2. The leader will be the auctioneer and can begin with any item on the sheet. It is best to pick the items at random rather than to proceed from top to bottom.

3. Before you begin, here are some further comments.

   (a) You are not limited in your bidding to the amounts you budgeted. During the auction you may decide to spend more and can do so providing the total amount never exceeds $4,000.

   (b) If you are the highest bidder for an item, that money is gone from your budget.

   (c) If you bid but do not win, that money can be used for other items or included in other bids.

   (d) Enter your top bid in the second column.

   (e) Enter the top bid the item commanded in the last column.

To the Leader:

Leader starts the auction with, "Who will give me $50 for _____?" If item is not popular, lower beginning bid to get auction started. Close bidding with, "Going once, going twice, sold to _____ for $_____." Keep bids in jumps of $25 or higher; otherwise the auction will drag.

4. Following the completion of all the bidding, the leader reads aloud the Values Key which identifies the values used in the different items.

Discussion: You may wish to compare the value areas for which you bid the highest or which you bought with the top five values you wrote down at the beginning. What similarities are there, if any, between the two? When you look at the amount you budgeted (column one) and the amount you actually bid (column two) what made you change? Consider the following questions:

Did you stick closely to the amount allotted? If not, why not?

Did you use up your resources before you could bid on later value areas? Why?

Were you reluctant to risk much consistently because you were afraid of using up your money too soon and thus lose out on valued items? Why?

How did you feel when you did not get a value you thought important?

What ideas did you get through this experience as to what you do about your values in your daily living? Think of the $4,000 as representing your whole life. How did you divide it?

To the Leader:

This exercise can be fun, but it also can generate lots of feeling and thinking. Allow plenty of time for discussion.

Values Bidding Tally Sheet

VALUES	Amount budgeted	Highest you bid	Winning bid
Success in your chosen field			
Satisfying and fulfilling marriage			
Freedom to do what you want			
Chance to be involved in the destinies of a nation			
Love and admiration of friends			
Faithfulness to a person, group, institution or political entity			
Self-confidence, a positive outlook on life, peace of mind			
Happy family life			
Recognition as an attractive person			
Long life free of illness			
Private library to satisfy your curiosity and learn what you want			
Satisfying religious faith			
Time and money to enjoy yourself			
Lifetime financial security			
Lovely home in a beautiful setting			
World where everyone is treated fairly			
Chance to eliminate sickness, poverty			
International recognition, popularity			
Good sense, judgment and insight			
Country free of graft, lying, cheating or stealing			
Freedom within your work setting			
Really close love relationship			
Being able to produce new forms, ideas			

Values Key

Value	Description for Values Bidding
Success	Success in your chosen field
Marriage	A satisfying and fulfilling marriage
Personal independence	Freedom to do what you want
Power	A chance to be involved in the destinies of a nation
Love, friendship, approval	The love and admiration of friends
Loyalty	Faithfulness to a person, group, institution or political entity
Emotional well-being	Self-confidence, a positive outlook, peace of mind
Family	A happy family life
Appearance	Recognition as a very attractive person
Health	A long life free of illness
Knowledge	A private library to satisfy your curiosity and learn anything you want
Religion	A satisfying religious faith
Pleasure	Time and money to enjoy yourself for a time
Security	Lifetime financial security
Aesthetic, achievement	A lovely home in a beautiful setting
Justice	A world where everyone is treated fairly
Altruism	A chance to eliminate sickness and poverty
Fame, approval	International recognition and popularity
Wisdom	Good sense, judgment and insight
Honesty	A country free of graft, lying, cheating and stealing
Work independence	Freedom within your work setting
Love	A really close love relationship
Creativity	Being able to produce new forms, ideas

IV. Setting Goals and Decision Making

A decision is a process that selects a problem to be solved and produces a number of alternatives from which a particular alternative is selected for implementation using values, priorities, and overcoming barriers. The exercises in this section provide skills and strategies for implementing each of these steps.

"To be able to choose the line of greatest advantage instead of yielding in the path of least resistance . . . is the essence of freedom."

George Bernard Shaw

exercise twelve: *60 minutes*

12   *Using Brainstorming To Make Decisions*

Purpose: To practice creative problem-solving as a group effort.

The following exercise explains the process of brainstorming which can be used to generate a large number of ideas or solutions or alternatives to a problem by suspending any criticism or evaluation. It is especially useful when group decisions are required.

Discussion: What is the effect on you when you are asked to volunteer ideas for critical evaluation before a group?

This sample experience can be used as a warm-up for a real problem-solving session.

Procedure:

1.   Form into small groups of six to eight and select a recorder. The recorder will list every idea generated by the group on either a sheet of paper or a chalkboard.

2.   The ground rules are: There will be no criticism or any evaluation, positive or negative, during the brainstorming phase. Far-out ideas are encouraged as they may trigger other more practical ideas. Quantity is desired.

3.   Here is the problem to be solved:

You are all members of the Board of Directors for a company which manufactures bathtubs. Because of increasing water shortages and a slow-down in new housing starts, your company finds itself with an excess inventory of one million bathtubs. It is up to you to think of other ways to use bathtubs so that your company can tap new markets.

(You have 5 minutes.)

4. Now evaluate your ideas by grouping them into categories. An example would be:

> Simple
> Hard
> Difficult to accomplish

(Another category might fit your ideas better.)

5. The next step is to develop criteria or values by which to select the best of the category. To help develop values or criteria, you might think of —

> Effect on ultimate goal
>
> Possible effect on other people
>
> Long-range effect on costs (initial cost, upkeep, resale, etc.)
>
> Effect on opinion (aesthetic, reputation, attitude)
>
> Effect on time (present, later, by stages)

6. Rank order the criteria according to which is most important to you, your company or agency.

7. Select one decision or combination of decisions and develop a plan of action. You can use the method described on page 52.

(The whole process of brainstorming is discussed at great length in book edited by Angelo M. Biondi. *)

*Angelo M. Biondi, editor, *The Creative Process* (Buffalo, New York, D. O. K. Publishers, Inc., 1972).

exercise thirteen: *60 minutes*

13   *Rational Steps To Decision-Making*

Purpose: To develop a rational system for making decisions.

People make decisions in a variety of ways. They may ask experts to make their decisions for them, make decisions according to superstition or through habit, or leave decision-making to chance. A better way is to follow certain rational steps.

Discussion: Think of a decision you made recently. What style do <u>you</u> ordinarily use in making decisions? Can you analyze any steps you followed?

Procedure: Rational steps in making a decision are:

1. Defining the problem —

   (a) State the problem. (Example: Shall I ask my roommate to move?)

   (b) Ask why? (Example of answer: She is messy, inconsiderate, doesn't do her share.)

   (c) Restate the problem. (Example: In what ways can I try to get my roommate to be more liveable?)

   (d) Write the restated problem on the worksheet.

2. At top of worksheet, list the five values most important to you — either from your values exercises or some values you think of now.

3. Alternatives — List all of the possible ways of solving the problem on the worksheet. List even those ways you will only give passing consideration. Ask the others in your group to help you think of other alternatives. (Brainstorm)

4. Information — What facts do you need to know? (Example: How much would it cost to live alone? Are there any other apartments available that you can afford? Where do you find this information?) You may need to gather information before you can go on to the next steps.

5. List any reasons you can think of <u>for</u> each alternative.

6. List any reasons you can think of <u>against</u> each alternative.

7. List values each alternative will accommodate. Are any of them the values you listed at the top of the page? Mark a plus (+) beside them.

8. One reason many people do not follow through on decisions is that they cannot be sure of the outcome and are afraid to risk. Trying to foresee all possible outcomes both good and bad for each alternative is one way to lessen the risk. List them on your worksheet.

9. Ask the members of your small group to brainstorm ways to overcome or reduce negative outcomes. List the ways.

10. Write down decision or solution that is most satisfying to you in terms of values, outcomes and risk-taking.

Discussion: Share your decision with your small group. How will you carry it out. What is the first step? The following exercise-plan-of-action will help with this step. Other group members may have suggestions for you. When will you take it? Be specific and set a date. After all members of your group answer the above questions to their satisfaction, write the answers on the worksheet.

Once a decision is made, learn to live with it and do not continue to weigh the same issues.

To the Leader:

If information-gathering is necessary for reaching a final decision, the leader may wish to do the exercise through Step 2 during the first session, assign Step 3 as homework and complete the exercise at another session.

References

Other effective methods for decision-making are described in the following:

Carkhuff, Robert. *The Art of Problem Solving*. Amherst, Mass.: Human Resources Development Press, 1973.

Gelatt, H. B., Varenhorst, Barbara and Carey, Richard, *Deciding*. New York: College Entrance Examination Board, 1972.

Parnes, Sidney J., *Creative Behavior Guidebook*. New York: Charles Scribner & Sons, 1967.

Scholz, Nelle T., Prince, Judith S. and Miller, Gordon P., *How To Decide: A Guide for Women*. New York: College Entrance Examination Board, 1975.

Making A Decision

or

Doing My Own Thing

Worksheet

Problem:

Restated Problem:

Top Values:

1.
2.
3.
4.
5.

Alternatives	Reasons For	Reasons Against	Values Satisfied by Alternative	Possible Outcomes	How to Overcome Negative Outcomes
1.					
2.					
3.					

Decision or Solution:

What is your next step? (Be specific.)

When? (See Plan of Action)

Any Decision is One of a Series

exercise fourteen: *60 minutes*

Plan of Action   **14**

Purpose: To set up a step-by-step process for implementing a decision.

Reaching a decision is only a first step. For some people that is enough to start the action necessary to reach their goals. Most of us need to think through an orderly process before we achieve our goals. Trying to foresee as many obstacles as possible and thinking of ways to overcome them, helps to lower the risk factor. The following procedure attempts to describe one way.

Discussion: Can you think of some decision you made in the past that you never carried out? Why not? Was it lack of information? Didn't know where to start? Too risky?

Procedure:

1. List decision or objective you arrived at in previous exercise on worksheet.

2. List all obstacles you can anticipate. Are other people involved? costs? time?

3. List all the ways you can think of to overcome or manage the obstacles. Ask your group for other ideas. A fresh perspective really helps. (Brainstorm)

4. How long will it take you to reach your goal? Write the date in the proper space on the worksheet.

5. Follow the rest of the steps on the worksheet.

6. Set a date for group members to share with each other their progress on reaching their goals.

Discussion: Did laying out a plan affect your decision? Change or modify it? Does it seem more or less possible?

Plan of Action
Worksheet

1. Decision or objective ....

2. What, if anything, do you anticipate might make it especially
    difficult for you to achieve this goal?

    1st Obstacle   2nd Obstacle   3rd Obstacle

    ....

3. Ways to Manage   Ways to Manage   Ways to Manage

    ....

    ....

4. End result in .... (weeks, months, years)

5. What is the first step? ....

    ....

6. How do you do it? ....

    ....

    Where? ....

    Who? (Will you need other people to help?) ....

    ....

    What do you need? (materials, if any) ....

    ....

    Cost? ....

    Anything else? ....

7. When will you start? ....

    Most critical things you will do the first week:

    ....

    Most critical things to accomplish in first month:

    ....

    Most critical things to accomplish first six months:

    ....

7. (continued)

What will you have accomplished in one year?

....

In . . . . years, what will you have accomplished?

....

8.   Date to share progress with group ....

9.   Repeat from Step 5 if additional steps are needed.

....

....

....

....

....

....

....

....

....

V. Men-Women Relationships

Discussion and exercises of attitudes, problem areas, lifestyles and roles.
> Assumptions
> Attitudes Toward Women
> Separate But Equal
> Vignettes for Discussion
> Responsibility vs. Dependency

"The first responsibility of a 'liberated' woman is to lead the fullest, freest, and most imaginative life she can. The second responsibility is her solidarity with other women. She may live and work and make love with men. But she has no right to represent her situation as simpler, or less suspect, or less full of compromises than it really is. Her good relations with men must not be bought at the price of betraying her sisters."

Susan Sontag
(as quoted in "Toward a Woman-Centered University" by Adrienne Rich in *Chronicle of Higher Education*, July 21, 1975)

exercise fifteen: *30 minutes*

Assumptions   **15**

Purpose: To test the realities of certain assumptions which
may be influencing your behavior.

On a more personal level, both men and women often
base their behavior and goals on assumptions they believe
the opposite sex have about them. This exercise attempts to
test the reality of these assumptions.

Discussion: What do women believe that men look for in a woman?
What do men believe women desire and expect in a man?

Procedure:

1. If it is a mixed group, men and women form separate groups
   by sex. If group is one sex, have half the group answer the
   questions from point of view of men, half from point of view
   of women. (For example, in an all women workshop, ask —
   "If you were a man, with what kind of woman do you want to
   spend the rest of your life?" Try to put yourself in this role.

2. Each group discusses and reaches agreement on the following
   topic:

   "With what kind of woman (or man) do you want to spend
   the rest of your life?" Consider appearance, personality,
   behavior and character.

Discussion: Is this what you expected the other sex group to say?
What did you expect? Why did you expect this? How do you feel
about the other's expectations of your sex? Was your group's
final description similar to description in the original discussion
of how men like women to be, and vice versa?

To the Leader:

Leaders should preface instructions with a statement
clarifying purpose of exercise. The participants may
resist if they feel the leaders are assuming that all the
participants plan to follow the traditional lifestyle.

exercise sixteen: *45 minutes*

16   *Attitudes Toward Women*

Purpose: To expose myths and realities about the current
attitudes toward women in our society.

Most of us agree intellectually that men and women should
have equal treatment. However, since we are all part of the
same culture, both men and women have developed similar attitudes toward women. These attitudes cannot but help influence
our behaviors, our decisions and our goals. A way to reassess
these attitudes is to examine them and see if they fit with the
facts or are they, indeed, stereotyped ideas and myths?

Discussion: Can you think of a time when someone made a decision
involving you based on a stereotype rather than your own personal
qualifications? How did you feel about it?

Procedure: (See Worksheet)

To the Leader:

In large group (no larger than 16-20) any of the statements
can be the basis for a discussion. If group is too large to
permit everyone to speak, divide into smaller groups. In
this case, a group of ten or so would give a variety of
opinions and information. Ask each person volunteering
an opinion to back it with facts. Most people will give as
evidence a personal experience. It would be a good idea
for the leader to be prepared with data from current literature, Civil Rights laws, etc.

Discussion: Which statement do you want to talk about? Did you
agree? Disagree? Why? What evidence do you have to support
your opinion? Are there any statements you would like to discuss in order to clarify your own thoughts or to find out the
opinions of others?

Attitudes Toward Women
Worksheet

Procedure: For each statement, please indicate in the blank to the left of the statement —

> SA — strongly agree
>
> A — tend to agree
>
> D — tend to disagree
>
> SD — strongly disagree

.... 1.   Generally speaking, women gossip more than men do.

.... 2.   Women tend to quit their jobs more frequently than men do.

.... 3.   Men teachers are better disciplinarians than women teachers.

.... 4.   Most women tend to lose their femininity when they perform "masculine" jobs.

.... 5.   Women tend to respond emotionally, men by thinking.

.... 6.   Children usually suffer when mothers work outside the home.

.... 7.   Most women really do not like to work under other women.

.... 8.   Most men really do feel superior to women.

.... 9.   Most women really prefer a strong, dominating male.

.... 10.   Normal women find their greatest fulfillment at home as good wives and mothers.

.... 11.   Women who work are taking jobs away from men.

.... 12.   Birth control information and devices should be readily available to any female over age fourteen who requests them.

.... 13.   Marriage is an institution that primarily benefits males.

.... 14.   Industry and large school systems, etc., should provide free child care in order to enable mothers to continue working or preparing for a career.

.... 15.   To make up for past discrimination, women should receive preference in promotions and hiring until the male-female ratio is balanced.

exercise seventeen: *40 minutes*

17   *Separate But Equal*

Purpose: To place ourselves in decision-making positions to see
          if our own attitudes toward women affect these decisions.

Discussion: Running a home and having a career obviously present
                problems. These are dual roles expected of most women. Dis-
                cuss some problems that might affect your career or home life.

Procedure:

  1. Each of you is an executive in a large company with a great
     deal of responsibility for the growth and productivity of your
     company. You have learned from experience that it is im-
     portant to pick the right person for a middle management job
     — a person with time, energy and a commitment to the company.

  2. Your leader will hand you a memo which concerns a decision
     you must make concerning one of your employees.

  3. Write your decision at the bottom of the memo.

Discussion: Why did you make the decision you did? What attitudes
                or stereotypes does this show as to how much confidence you
                have in men as compared to women in combining marriage and
                career? Were your expectations different for a man employee
                than for a woman employee?

To the Leader:

                There are two memos on the next page for each of three
                different situations. Distribute one memo to each participant.
                When they have finished, have all the participants who re-
                ceived Memo No. 1 share their decisions. Proceed to
                Memo No. 1A then Memo No. 2 and 2A and so on. After the
                sharing, follow the discussion model above.

                (This exercise is taken from a survey of 1,500 male
                executives who responded to hypothetical memos from
                married employees. *)

*Benson Rosen, Thomas H. Jerdee, Thomas L. Prestwick, ''Dual-Career Marital Adjustment: Potential Effects
of Discriminatory Managerial Attitude,'' in *Journal of Marriage and the Family*. Vol. 37, No. 3, 1975. pp.
565-572.

Memos for Discussion

Memo #1

Karen Wood, age 35, married, with four children, wishes to be considered for the job of purchasing manager. This position has just been vacated. One of the requirements of the job is that it involves up to 20 days of travel a month.

( )   I recommend Karen be hired for the position.

( )   I recommend Karen not be hired for the position.

Memo #1-A

Karl Wood, age 35, married, with four children, wishes to be considered for the job of purchasing manager. This position has just been vacated. One of the requirements of the job is that it involves up to 20 days of travel a month.

( )   I recommend Karl be hired for the position.

( )   I recommend Karl not be hired for the position.

Memo #2

Jack Garrison, freelance writer, husband of Judy Garrison, aspiring manager, complains bitterly after attending an executive cocktail party. Judy explains that she is ambitious and these functions are necessary for the advancement of her career.

( )   Jack should attend and stop making an issue of it as it helps Judy's career.

( )   Judy should go to such parties alone even though this would be socially awkward.

Memo #2-A

Judy Garrison, freelance writer, wife of Jack Garrison, aspiring manager, complains bitterly after attending an executive cocktail party. Jack explains that he is ambitious and these functions are necessary for the advancement of his career.

( )   Judy should attend and stop making an issue of it as it helps Jack's career.

( )   Jack should go to such parties alone even though this would be socially awkward.

Memo #3

Sally Davis, who is up for promotion, has announced that her primary duty is toward her family and she expects to balance her time accordingly. She is one of our most competent employees and capable of handling even more responsibility in the new job.

( )   I agree to promote her.

( )   I do not agree to promote her.

Memo #3-A

Samuel Davis, who is up for promotion, has announced that his primary duty is toward his family and he expects to balance his time accordingly. He is one of our most competent employees and capable of handling even more responsibility in the new job.

( )   I agree to promote him.

( )   I do not agree to promote him.

Memo #4

Rachel Cooper, a computer operator, has played a key role in computerizing the company's inventory. Recently, her husband was offered an attractive managerial position with a large retail organization on the West Coast. They are seriously considering the move. Rachel has been told she has a bright future with the organization and it would be a shame if she pulled out just as they are expanding.

( )   I should try to convince Rachel that she has too much invested in her career to leave now.

( )   The decision should be hers. I would not try to influence her.

Memo #4-A

Richard Cooper, a computer operator, has played a key role in computerizing the company's inventory. Recently, his wife was offered an attractive managerial position with a large retail organization on the West Coast. They are seriously considering the move. Richard has been told he has a bright future with the organization and it would be a shame if he pulled out just as they are expanding.

( )   I should try to convince Richard that he has too much invested in his career to leave now.

( )   The decision should be his. I would not try to influence him.

The results of the survey by Rosen, Jerdee and Prestwick showed that in every situation the executive respondent proved more willing to indulge and help men than women. For example, in Memos 1 and 1A, the male applicant was evaluated as better suited for the job and more likely to remain with the company. Moreover, a majority of the executives felt it inappropriate to hire a woman for a job requiring extensive travel.

Memos 2 and 2A: Fewer than half of the executives felt that Jack should attend future cocktail parties and "stop making an issue of it." Thirty-eight percent felt Judy should go to such parties alone "even though this would be socially awkward." When the roles were reversed and the complaining spouse was the wife, sixty-nine percent of the executives felt she was obliged to go; only seventeen percent believed that Jack should go to the parties alone.

Memos 3 and 3A: Only 42 percent of the executives agreed to promote Sally. When they evaluated the same memo for Samuel, however, 55 percent gave him the nod. The authors suggest that a man who indicates devotion to family may be perceived as a wholesome, well-rounded individual while a woman with the same feelings is perceived as lacking loyalty and commitment to the firm.

Memos 4 and 4A: Organizational efforts to retain the computer operator were viewed as significantly more appropriate for a male than for a female employee. When the husband in a dual-career marriage had an opportunity to move for a better job, his wife, even though a highly-valued employee, was expected to give up her own job for the sake of his career.

exercise eighteen: *30-60 minutes*

18   *Vignettes for Discussion*

Purpose: To explore various solutions to a conflict of roles.

Roles for men and women are changing. Many young people
are re-examining cultural expectations of their roles with
resulting confusion and upheaval. Below are some vignettes
of situations where conflicts of roles occur. A discussion of
various solutions can help many persons to clarify their own
roles. There is no correct solution. Every person must consider values, goals, self-concepts to arrive at a satisfactory
role.

Discussion: Can you think of any situation with your family,
friends, boyfriend, or school peer group where it was obvious
for you that you were expected to behave or decide in a traditional
pattern? What did you do? How did you feel?

Procedure: Read some of the vignettes below. What is your
reaction to each of the solutions? What is gained from the
solution? What is given up? What are the long-range effects?

Vignette #1:

Laura has always dreamed of being an architect. Her high school
notebooks were full of house plans, doorway details and new light
fixtures. She built a model house for the science fair. She is in
her second year at the university. She has heard comments that
architecture is a 'man's field.' She is often the only woman in
class. She senses that some of her male classmates think she
might be better off studying home economics. Recently, one of
the university forum speakers was a well-known educator whose
theme was that men and women should be educated in different
ways for different things. Laura is wondering — should she
change to interior decorating?

Vignette #2:

Ann is attractive, well-liked, clever, vivacious — and smart. She makes superior grades, carries a heavy load of extra-curricular activities and works part-time in the dean's office. Recently, she has been dating Dave. She has noticed how much better things go when he makes the decisions, directs the conversation, and 'leads out.' On the night after the President's talk, she tried to discuss the speech with Dave (the international situation and America's role in the world). He was not responsive and finally closed the conversation by saying, "Ann, you're too smart for your own good."

Vignette #3:

Gail packed her suitcase for the weekend with Bob feeling a mixture of anticipation and guilt. Her midwestern family and church background had not prepared her for this. Although more sophisticated now in her junior year about the relativities of the so-called Christian virtues of honesty, chastity, temperance, etc., she still could not shake off uneasiness about this plan to drive to a motel in the mountains. Of course, a lot of the other girls had been sleeping with their fiances and it was not as though she were not going to marry Bob someday. They had talked it over soberly. They knew they loved each other but they could not marry for at least three years if Bob got his hoped-for appointment to the Naval Academy. Gail's misgivings had been overcome quite unexpectedly when she found out that her best friend and fellow "Y" Board member had faced the same problem a year ago and had no regrets. Well, the die was cast. She snapped the lock of her suitcase.

Vignette #4:

Carol has reached the end of her sophomore year and must decide on her major. She has a chance to take an honors program with a focus on chemistry which greatly intrigues her. But it will mean a heavy program of reading and research and probably graduate studies. Carol is also active in student activities and has a "steady" boyfriend who is urging her to get married soon. If she marries, she feels she should take a lighter course and also one which will fit her to get a job and help her husband through graduate school. She decides that since marriage is her goal and she will only be working for a short time, she will switch to a general course and take typing and shorthand as electives.

Vignette #5:

"You're a real dope if you give up the fellowship," scolded Jean. "Here is your chance to prove that women as well as men can make good in the sciences. You may never have such a good opportunity again! Surely Alec can't expect you to do this." Ann patted her friend's arm reassuringly, "Now, now, don't get excited. Nobody's doing me dirt. I've thought it all through very carefully and I must say my toughest problem has been convincing Alec. You see, it's this way. Alec is going to be a great man in his field. I feel it in my bones. It's going to be exciting to work with him and help him get started. Somehow, I don't feel the need to get a Ph.D. in science. I can use my skill and interests in a supplementary way, in holding down a lab job and in helping Alec with his experiments. We are going to have a wonderful life together. Don't, for goodness'sake, sound as though I'm giving up something."

exercise nineteen: *50 minutes*

19   *Responsibility versus Dependency*

Purpose: To help you discover your potential for taking responsibility.

In your relationships with other people — friends, spouse, boss, teachers — you act dependently sometimes and sometimes independently. Perhaps you are more often one than the other. Perhaps your style of acting one way or the other has unknown effects on the other person. Do you take on unnecessary responsibilities? The following exercise helps clarify your feelings about each role, your style and some of the consequences.

Discussion: Do you think of yourself as an independent person? Dependent? Are you sometimes dependent and sometimes independent — different in different situations with different people? Do you have any concern about the way you perform in either role?

Procedure:

1. This is a non-verbal exercise (no talking). Pick a partner from your support group. During the exercise, try to be aware of your feelings.

2. One of the pair keeps her eyes closed while the other person leads her around the room, into the corridor, over, under or around obstacles, for 10 minutes.

3. Your leader will tell you when the 10 minutes are up. When she signals, reverse roles.

4. Now pick a different partner. Someone you don't know well, from another support group.

5. Repeat above procedure. Remember, this is a non-verbal exercise.

Discussion: In small groups, discuss —

Did you like taking the lead? Was it a burden? Did the time seem to pass slowly or quickly? How did your partner like being led by you? Were you over-protective? Did you give her freedom to move? How did it feel being completely responsible for someone else?

How did it feel being completely dependent on another person? Did you behave here the same as you do in other situations outside the group?

You might want to try this exercise outside the group with a member of the opposite sex to see if your reactions are different. What did you learn about yourself?

VI. Planning for Contingencies of the Future

Simulations to anticipate possible events in order to be more realistically prepared.

Simulations of a traditional-life style to isolate stress periods in order to plan ameliorative measures.

Traditional Life Style

Alternatives or Is There a Paradise?

"*A woman can be ailing conveniently, or be extravagant conveniently, and society will put up with her; but if she puts her career aims even on a parity with her husband's, she is in difficulty.*"
David Riesman

exercise twenty: *60 minutes*

Traditional Lifestyle 20

Purpose: To understand the pressures and conflicts of marriage and parenthood.

Rarely do young people arrive at marriage and parenthood with adequate preparation for the strains and pressures ahead. In spite of interest in alternate lifestyles, the majority of young people will eventually opt for a traditional marriage. This exercise aims to have each sex understand the pressures and conflicts of their roles and to prepare for these pressures.

Discussion: What satisfactions and dissatisfactions do you feel your parents get from their marriage? How did it get this way? Forty percent of American marriages end in divorce. Let's look at some of the pressures that may cause this.

Procedure: Ask for volunteers to role-play a college or high school junior and her boyfriend, very much in love, planning on marriage. Ask them to stand close to each other to demonstrate their feelings toward each other.

Progress through the following life stages adding other members of the group to the family when necessary. At each stage, have participants place themselves in the physical positions that would demonstrate their relationship to each other. The leader and/or other participants can ask each role player, "How do you feel now?" "Why did you move that way?" and finally, when appropriate, "Can you think of anything that you could do to improve your situation." (Leader reads the following script.)

1. Young newlyweds: Both are working; wife also does housework and cooking; husband helps with dishes, puts out garbage.

   (At each step, participants position themselves in a way to show their feelings; for example, arms around each other to show closeness.)

2. First child: Wife quits her job to have the baby; husband works. (Another participant becomes the baby and positions herself to show helplessness and closeness to either parent.)

3. <u>Second child</u>: Wife, full-time housewife now; new house; husband promoted, more responsibility at work. (Add another participant.)

4. <u>Third child</u>: All three children are pre-school age; husband moving up in company, travels, away for meetings, etc. All five members of family position themselves to show relationship to each other, keeping in mind age and activities at this stage.

5. <u>School age children</u>: Husband still more successful; wife expected to entertain for company. Children elementary school level. Participants change positions to reflect new stage.

6. <u>Teenage children</u>: Conflicts between husband and wife over children — late hours, drinking, drugs, sloppiness, laziness. Husband now a vice-president of his company. (Participants rearrange themselves to show new relationships.)

7. <u>Empty nest</u>: Children now away either at college or married. (Three children participants depart leaving husband and wife alone.)

8. <u>Aged parents</u>: One parent is in need of care.

Discussion: Have each participant express feelings and reactions to role playing. How does this fit their own personal goals? What could you do that would help you through a stressful period? Is there anything you can do now that would help alleviate a stressful period later? (Other lifestyles may be the solution for you but they are also not without problems.)

To the Leader:

1. This exercise has proven especially interesting and worthwhile in groups with low levels of "consciousness-raising" or mixed groups (mixed by sex and/or awareness). For women who already see themselves as independent and have thought through their marriage goals, this exercise is irrelevant.

2. This exercise can also be used in men-women relationships.

3. The next topic on planning for contingencies of the future follows. It leads naturally from this exercise.

exercise twenty-one: *2 hours*

Alternatives — or Is There a Paradise? *   **21**

Purpose: To explore some of the potential stresses and strains
of alternative life styles.

While role-playing a traditional lifestyle can focus on
the stresses and conflicts that arise, you may decide you will
be different and thus avoid the conflicts your parents suffered.
However, no one lifestyle guarantees paradise. This exercise
aims to give young people a greater awareness of the realities
of life. Of course, no one can foresee all the circumstances
that may arise but being aware of alternatives and planning
for them gives a person greater self-confidence and experience
when, and if, expected hardship occurs. Hopefully, some of
you may be motivated to rethink your current activities and
plans in order to minimize or avoid future pitfalls.

To the Leader:

1. It is the task of the group to work on the problem
with the participant. Group responsibility makes
discussion easier, generates more ideas, creates
a mutual helping atmosphere and gives all the
participants six to ten experiences in problem-
solving and identification with other possible "lives"
even though each has only one chance factor.

2. The leader should point out, when appropriate:
An unskilled divorced mother who needs employment
usually cannot find child-care facilities or housing
at a price she can afford; a full-time homemaker
does not need to wait until her children are grown
to continue her education — she can go to school
while they are in school; forty years of age is not
too late to start a college education, a career or
fulfilling activity since, on the average, she will
live 35 more years.

_____

*Idea from Advisory Commission on the Status of Women, State of California, 1972.

3. Homework for fact-gathering may be necessary and desirable. For example, finding out and reporting back on the availability and cost of the various kinds of child care, what jobs and salaries are listed in help-wanted ads they could do, whether public transportation is available to specific listings, what are current housing costs, college or technical school costs, etc.

Discussion: Statistics from the U.S. Department of Labor show:

You will probably live to be 75 years of age.
You will probably marry.
You will have almost 50 years of life after your youngest child enters school.
Nine out of ten women are employed sometime during their lives.
Six out of ten women will work fulltime for up to thirty years.
Four out of ten women will be divorced.
One in ten will be widowed before she is 50.

Were you aware of these facts? Any surprises?

Procedure: Keeping in mind the above facts, go around the group one at a time and —

1. Share with your group your goals for education, career, marriage and family.

2. On the following pages there are a number of "Chance Factors" described. Pick one and read it to your group.

   (Note to Leader: Some of these Chance Factors may be typed on slips of paper, then folded so that the participant makes a "chance" selection.)

3. All of you in the support group now help the participant deal with the problem described until she arrives at a solution which is satisfactory and feasible to her.

   Repeat the procedure with each member of the group.

Discussion: After each person reaches a solution, can you — as a group — think of ways this situation could have been avoided or eased by early preparation?

Chance Factors

Scenario #1

You "fall into" a dream job soon after graduation from college and three years later meet and marry a young man with a promising future in another field from yours. You keep on working after your two children are born because you love your work and you are rising fast in the company. Eight years later when you are near the top, the whole firm moves to New York and you are offered the directorship. There are no opportunities for you at your level in your field at another company in town. Meanwhile, your husband has already risen in his profession locally and opportunities for him in New York are not promising. What should you do?

Scenario #2

When you are only 34, your husband is tragically killed in an automobile accident. Your children are four, eight and ten. There is some life insurance but only enough to last six months at your current scale of living. How will you cope?

Scenario #3

You drop out of school before you graduate to marry your boy-friend. He still has two years to go, so you get a job as a clerk-typist in a law firm to put him through college. He graduates and gets a good job. Soon after, you are promoted to head secretary in the law firm. You enjoy the work and are interested in the cases being handled. However, after fifteen years you find your secretarial role less and less challenging. Even though you both wanted children, none have come along and you decide not to adopt since you are both enjoying the freedom. You are 38. What will you do with the rest of your life?

Scenario #4

You dropped out of college after one semester to marry. However, it became apparent after two years of marriage that it was a mistake and you were divorced. You remarry when you are 24 and have two children. When you are 35, your husband's job and whole field of work are wiped out by automation. Your children are seven and nine. What will you do?

Scenario #5

Your father dies unexpectedly when you are 19 and your mother is in poor health. You have four younger brothers and sisters — the youngest being only two years old. The support of the family is now up to you. You must drop out of school and, since you have no practical skills and jobs are scarce, you get work in a cleaning plant. The pay is not bad but you are pretty tired by night, especially after seeing to things at home. How can you plan the rest of your life?

Scenario #6

You meet your husband while you are both enrolled in a Ph.D. program. You both continue in school and you work for several years as a professional woman. You want children, but you recognize the realities of dividing your time between home and a profession. What are your alternatives?

Scenario #7

Your fiance graduates from college when you finish your junior year and he is offered a good job in a town which has no four-year college. You marry and go with him. When you are 38 and your children are 14 and 16, your husband says he wants a divorce to marry a younger woman. Under no-fault divorce law, he can do this and there is nothing you can do about it. The new law also says that you cannot get alimony (now known as spousal support) just because you are a woman, but since you have been married for such a long time the court awards you a small amount of "spousal support" for three years and child support until the children are 18. You also get one of the cars and the furniture, which are paid for, and the house which is only half paid for. Even with support money, there is not going to be enough to make ends meet. How will you cope?

Scenario #8

In your senior year at college, you fall madly in love with an exciting "older man of 31" who is already successful in business. He is of the firm opinion that a woman's place is in the home and often states, "No wife of mine will ever work." You marry and continue to be generally compatible, but over the years his business affairs take up more and more of his time. He also prefers spending his leisure time "with the boys" hunting and fishing. Your children are all off on their own by the time you are 42 years old. What do you do with the rest of your life?

Scenario #9

After working for a year, you marry at the age of 19. You enjoy 20 years of homemaking but when you are 40 your children are all grown and busy with their own lives. You do not want to just sit home for another 35 years. What can you do?

Scenario #10

When you are 19, you go to work for a large oil company. Two years later you marry a handsome, dashing driller and by the time you are 26 you have four children. Your husband is assigned to work in remote places, is home less and less, starts playing around with other women and doesn't send money home regularly for you and the family. You try for three years to straighten things out, but at the age of 32 you realize things are worse than ever and you get a divorce. The court awards you some alimony (now known as spousal support) and child support, but it is not enough to live on and there is very little community property — just furniture and clothing. What can you do?

Scenario #11

You marry during your last year of college and go to work immediately after graduation so that your husband can finish. After he graduates, you both spend two years teaching abroad. When you return, you become pregnant and spend the year doing substitute teaching while your husband gets his master's degree. During the second year in his program, you continue teaching part-time. You enjoy being a mother and begin to develop some of the creative talent you have not previously had time for. Reluctantly you commit yourself to go with your husband as he begins his Ph.D. program but you find yourself increasingly dissatisfied with his total academic involvement and frustrated by the fact that there is not enough money for you to be in school. You leave the marriage, taking the child with you. What are some of the multitude of decisions you must now face? and what will you do?

Scenario #12

You work for four years after graduating from college and then you meet a rugged, exciting fellow worker. He is obviously on the way up, a hard worker, a demanding supervisor, sometimes brusque but charming nevertheless. You marry and for a few months things are fine but then one night after an evening of heavy drinking, you quarrel and he beats you. You are shocked but cannot believe it will happen again. You even rationalize that you may have provoked him. After five years of marriage

and two children, you are wondering how you can continue. The
drinking and beatings have been getting more frequent; once your
arm was broken. It is beginning to affect the children and you
are all terrified most of the time. You are afraid some day you
may be seriously hurt. You are ashamed to tell your family.
They are old and have no room in their small apartment for
your family. The one time you called the police, they told you
it was a family argument and there was nothing they could do.
What do you do?

Scenario #13

You go to college erratically, dropping in and out to travel or
work. You finally get your degree and, while traveling, you
meet a man who really seems in tune with you. Having experienced
your own independence, you are reluctant to give it up for marriage
which he is pressing. What are some of your alternatives?

Scenario #14

A few months after graduating from high school you marry your
one and only boyfriend. You now have three children aged seven,
ten and twelve. You are 30 years old. Now that the children are
all in school, you have more time than you had before and you
begin trying some things you never had a chance to in the past.
You are taking some classes at the community college, making
new and interesting friends, becoming involved in a whole new
world of ideas and activities you never knew existed. More and
more, life at home seems dull and boring. You resent the time
you must spend there and feel the family is holding you back
from expressing and fulfilling yourself. You feel you deserve
to be happy, too? What do you do?

Scenario #15

You get pregnant before finishing high school, marry, and then
graduate. Your marriage has had its ups and downs but on the
whole has been satisfactory. You have raised four children who
are now off with young families of their own. You have been
married for 35 years and with the expenses of raising a family
have not been able to save more than $1,200 and a paid-up home
mortgage. Your husband dies suddenly of a heart attack. You
find that you cannot collect his Social Security widow's pension
until you are 60. You are now 52. You have never worked, have
had no training and cannot qualify for welfare because you own
your own home. You could sell the house, but it only costs you
$80 a month for upkeep and taxes and you know you cannot find
another place to live that cheaply. Your children are struggling
to make ends meet with their own families. What do you do?

VII. Role Models

Getting to know successful career women, to learn about their careers, their peak decisions, their problems; enlarging options; learning about other women's life styles.
> If She Can Do It, So Can I
> I Can Do Anything
> Women Who Have Achieved

"Children are educated by what the grown-up is and not by his talk."

Carl A. Jung
(Psychological Reflections, edited by
Jolande Jacobs, page 126)

exercise twenty-two: *variable time*

22   *"If She Can Do It, So Can I!"*

Purpose: To acquaint you with successful women career models.

Many young women complain that they do not know any women who are successful in the field in which they are interested. They wonder if it is possible for a woman to succeed in that particular field. What kind of woman can succeed? Can they identify with her? What problems did she have? Would she be helpful?

While this is not an exercise or strategy, it is included here because members in every workshop have asked to meet with role models in their field. This can be handled in different ways depending on the size of your group and the time you have. Below are a few suggestions. Your group can probably think of more.

Procedure:

1. Contact successful business and professional women in the community and ask if they would be willing to meet with a participant individually to talk about their careers.

2. Invite a group of business and professional women whose career fields correspond to the interests of the group to come to one session to respond to questions and share their experiences.

3. If the workshop group is too small, plan a session open to the public or to other interested groups.

To the Leader:

It is usually best to be ready with a few questions to start things rolling. The most frequently asked questions are —

1. What kind of preparation did you need for your job?

2. What are your relations with your male peers, those above and those below?

3. How do you manage your family and social life?

4. How long did it take you to get to the top and what were the circumstances?

5. What obstacles did you have to overcome?

Where To Find Role-Models in Your Community

1. Yellow pages of the Telephone Directory under listings by profession.

2. Members of the following organizations are involved in a wide range of careers. Names and addresses of the officers in local chapters are usually listed in the reference section of your local public library.

> Altrusa
> American Association of University Women
> American Business Women
> Business and Professional Women
> Pilot Club
> Quota Club
> Soroptimist Club
> Zonta Club

3. There may be a local chapter of one of the national professional organizations listed in the section on Women's Organizations, Business and Professional, in your community. Check the reference section of your public library.

exercise twenty-three:

"I Can Do Anything!"   23

Purpose: To expand your awareness of potential careers for women.

There are very few feminine role models in the "non-traditional" careers. While this is slowly changing, most women are still going into the "feminine" fields of teaching, nursing, social work, etc. One reason is that so many women are unaware of other choices open to them. On page 79 there is an exercise which lists occupations that may increase your options.

Procedure: Complete the "I Can Do Anything" exercise.

Discussion: Which occupations would you like to find out more about? Where would you go to find out more about them?

One of the best ways to learn about an occupation is to talk to women already working in the field. On page 77 is a list of sources that might help you locate these women. Other sources of information are listed in the reference section below.

According to the latest Department of Labor statistics, the highest paying fields are those traditionally considered male. Moreover, because of affirmative action laws, most firms in these fields are actively recruiting women.

To the Leader:

If the group has already done value clarification, they can discuss whether or not the occupation that interests each participant fits her values. If they have not done values clarification, they may wish to consider that next.

Some References

Occupational Outlook Handbook, U.S. Department of Labor, Dept. of Labor Statistics, Washington, D.C.: U.S. Govt. Printing Office, 1974-1975.

Dictionary of Occupational Titles, U.S. Department of Labor Manpower Administration, Washington, D.C.: U.S. Govt. Printing Office, 1965.

Chronical Guidance Publications, Inc. Moravia, New York, 1974. (File of descriptions of occupations.)

Careers For Women in the 70's, U.S. Department of Labor (Women's Bureau), Washington, D.C.: U.S. Govt. Printing Office, 1973.

Second Careers for Women, by Jane D. Fairbanks & Helen L. Bryson. P.O. Box 9660, Stanford, California: Second Careers for Women, 1975.

I Can Be Anything, by Joyce Mitchell, New York: College Entrance Examination Board, 1975.

Non-Traditional Careers for Women, by Sarah Splaver, New York: Julian Messner, 1974.

"Why Would a Girl Go Into Medicine?", by Margaret Campbell, M.D., Old Westbury, New York: The Feminist Press, 1973.

Matching College Women to Jobs, by J. L. Angel, New York: Simon & Schuster, 1970.

From College Girl to Working Woman: 201 Big City Jobs for Girl Graduates, by Susan Cowan, New York: Collier, 1970.

Corporate Lib: Women's Challenge to Management, by Eli Ginzberg. Baltimore, Md.: J. Hopkins Univ. Press, 1973.

I Can Do Anything
Worksheet

(1) Look at the list of occupations below and write "M" in the blank following the occupation if your <u>first</u> reaction is that it is a Man's field. Write "F" if your <u>first</u> reaction is that it is a woman's field. There are no right or wrong answers.

Occupation	M/F	Occupation	M/F
accountant	____	language interpreter	____
actuarist	____	law enforcement officer	____
advertising executive	____	lawyer	____
aerospace engineer	____	librarian	____
architect	____	manager, business	____
archaeologist	____	mathematician	____
army major	____	medical technologist	____
artist	____	mechanical engineer	____
banker	____	minister	____
biologist	____	museumologist	____
biomedical engineer	____	musician	____
botanist	____	naval ensign	____
buyer	____	nurse	____
chemist	____	nutritionist	____
city manager	____	pharmacist	____
civil engineer	____	photographer	____
chiropracter	____	physical therapist	____
clothing designer	____	physician	____
college professor	____	physicist	____
community planner	____	politician	____
computer programmer	____	priest	____
conductor	____	producer, film	____
dean	____	psychologist	____
dentist	____	public school administrator	____
dietician	____	occupational therapist	____
editor	____	oceanographer	____
elementary teacher	____	optometrist	____
electrical engineer	____	rabbi	____
flight attendant	____	realtor	____
forester	____	recreation director	____
funeral director	____	reporter	____
guidance counselor	____	secretary	____
insurance salesperson	____	social worker	____
interior designer	____	speech therapist	____
IRS investigator	____	statistician	____
high school teacher	____	technical writer	____
historian	____	veterinarian	____

(2) Put an asterisk (*) next to the occupations that have not occurred to you for yourself before.

(3) Put a plus sign (+) next to the occupations that interest you.

exercise twenty-four: *60-120 minutes*

24   *Women Who Have Achieved*

Purpose: To study the life stories of some well-known successful career women.

Your group may wish to read and discuss some books about women who have had successful, fulfilling lives either in paying careers or in other roles. Reading about their problems and solutions will help you become aware of some of the decisions you may have to face as well as learning that women can and do have successful careers as architects, engineers, industrial engineers, construction workers, etc.

Procedure: Read a book about a woman active in a field that interests you. The following bibliography lists many autobiographies and biographies about women. Librarians will also help you find other sources if you cannot find what you want on this list. There are many other books available. Don't hesitate to add your own.

Discussion: You might want to use the questions below to guide a discussion of your role model in the group.

How did this woman achieve her goal?

What obstacles, if any, were in her way?

How did she handle family and career?

What satisfactions did she enjoy?

What sacrifices did she have to make?

Career Women
Bibliography

Agress, Eliyahu. *Golda Meir*. Israel: Sabra Books, 1970.

Angelou, Maya. *I Know Why The Caged Bird Sings*. N.Y.: Random House, 1969.

Anticaglia, Elizabeth. *12 American Women*. Chicago: Nelson-Hall, 1975.

Auriol, Jacqueline. *I Live To Fly*. N.Y.: Dutton, 1970.

Bailey, Pearl. *The Raw Pearl*. N.Y.: Harcourt Brace & World, 1968.

Beauvoir, Simone De. *All Said And Done*. N.Y.: Putnam, 1974.

Benetar, Judith. *Admissions: Notes From a Woman Psychiatrist*. N.Y.: Charterhouse, 1974.

Brownmiller, Susan. *Shirley Chisholm: A Biography*. Garden City, N.J.: Doubleday, 1970.

Buckmaster, Henrietta. *Women Who Shaped History*. N.Y.: Collier Books, 1966.

Burgess, Alan. *Daylight Must Come: The Story of a Courageous Woman Doctor in the Congo*. N.Y.: Delacorte, 1974.

Burke, John. *Winged Legend: The Story of Amelia Earhart*. N.Y.: Putnam, 1970.

Campion, N. R. *Look To This Day! The Lively Education of a Great Woman Doctor*. Boston: Little, Brown & Co., 1965.

Cate, Curtis. *George Sand*. Burlington, Mass.: Houghton Mifflin Co., 1975.

Chamberlin, Hope. *A Majority of Members; Women in the U.S. Congress*. N.Y.: Praeger, 1973.

Chicago, Judy. *Through the Flower: My Struggles as a Woman Artist*. Garden City, N.J.: Doubleday, 1973.

Chisholm, Shirley. *Unbought and Unbossed*. Burlington, Mass.: Houghton Mifflin Co., 1970.

Cintron, Conchita. *Memoirs of a Bull Fighter*. N.Y.: Holt, Rinehart & Winston, 1968.

Cirile, Marie. *Detective Marie Cirile*. Garden City, N.J.: Doubleday, 1975.

Clarke, Robert. *Ellen Swallow; The Woman Who Founded Ecology*. Chicago: Follet, 1973.

Clymer, E. L. *Modern American Career Women*. N.Y.: Dodd, 1959.

Court, Margaret S. *Court On Court; A Life In Tennis*. N.Y.: Dodd, 1975.

Crawford, Deborah. *Lise Meitner; Atomic Pioneer*. N.Y.: Crown, 1969.

Dash, Joan. *A Life Of One's Own; Three Gifted Women And The Men They Married*. Hagerstown, Maryland: Harper & Row, 1973.

Davis, Allen J. *American Heroine; The Life and Legend of Jane Addams*. N.Y.: Oxford Univ. Press, 1973.

DeMille, Agnes. *Speak To Me, Dance With Me*. Boston: Little, Brown & Co., 1973.

Deutsch, Helene. *Confrontations With Myself; An Epilogue*. Scranton, Penna.: W. W. Norton & Co., 1973.

Duncan, Isadora. *My Life*. Garden City, N.J.: Doubleday, 1927.

Fiszroy, Nancy D. *Career Guidance For Women Entering Engineering*. Proceedings of an Engineering Foundation Conference, Henneker, N.H., New England College, 1973.

Fleming, A. M. *Great Women Teachers*. Philadelphia: J. P. Lippincott, 1965.

Flexner, Eleanor. *Mary Wollstonecraft*. N.Y.: Coward, McCann & Geoghehan, 1972.

Gibson, Althea. *I Always Wanted To Be Somebody*. Hagerstown, Maryland: Harper & Row, 1958.

Ginzberg, Eli. *Life Styles of Educated Women*. N.Y.: Columbia Univ. Press, 1966.

Goolagong, Evonne. *Evonne! On The Move*. N.Y.: Dutton, 1975.

Haefrich, Marcel. *Coco Chanel, Her Life, Her Secrets*. Boston: Little, Brown, & Co., 1972.

Hale, Nancy. *Mary Cassatt.* Garden City, N.J.: Doubleday & Co., 1975.

Hansberry, Lorraine. *To be Young, Gifted and Black.* Englewood Cliffs, N.J.: Prentice-Hall, 1969.

Hellman, Lillian. *An Unfinished Woman — A Memoir.* Boston: Little Brown, & Co., 1969.

Hoyt, Mary F. *American Women of the Space Age (Scientists).* N.Y.: Atheneum, 1966.

Joseph, Helen. *Tomorrow's Sun: A Smuggled Journal From South Africa.* N.Y.: John Day, 1967.

Lash, Joseph. *Eleanor, The Years Alone,* Scranton, Penna.: W. W. Norton, & Co., 1972.

MacLaine, Shirley. *You Can Get There From Here.* Scranton, Penna: W. W. Norton & Co., 1975.

Meir, Golda. *My Life.* N.Y.: Putnam, 1975.

Merriam, Eve. *Growing Up Female In America; Ten Lives.* Garden City, N.J.: Doubleday, 1971.

Mitford, Nancy. *Zelda, A Biography.* Hagerstown, Maryland: Harper & Row, 1970.

Millett, Kate. *Flying.* N.Y.: Knopf, 1974.

Neilson, Winthrop. *Seven Women: Great Painters.* Radnor, Penna.: Chilton Book Co., 1968.

Nin, Anais. *The Diary of Anais Nin.* Chicago: Swallow Press, 1966.

Singer, J. D. *My Mother, The Doctor.* N.Y.: Dutton, 1970.

Smaridge, Noral. *Famous British Novelists.* N.Y.: Dodd, 1967.

Stern, M. B. *We The Women: Career Firsts of 19th Century America.* N.Y.: Lennox Hill, 1975.

Tuft, Eleanor. *Our Hidden Heritage; Five Centuries of Women Artists.* N.Y.: Paddington, Press, 1974.

Seed, Suzanne. *Saturday's Child: 36 Women Talk About Their Jobs.* Chicago: Philip O'Hara Inc., 1973.

Wilson, D. C. *Lone Woman; The Story of Elizabeth Blackwell, The First Woman Doctor.* Boston: Little, Brown, & Co., 1970.

Yost, Edna. *Women of Modern Science.* N.Y.: Dodd, 1959.

Reference Books

Ireland, N. O. *Index To Women of the World; From Ancient to Modern Times.* Westwood, Mass.: Faxon Co., 1970.

James & Boyler (Eds.). *Notable American Women 1607-1950; A Biographical Dictionary.* 3 volumes. Cambridge, Mass.: Belknap Press of Harvard Univ., 1971.

VIII. Assertiveness Training

Involves expressing oneself without infringing upon the rights of another person. It is a direct, honest and appropriate expression of one's feelings and opinions. Assertive behavior is based on basic human rights, such as the right to say "no" without feeling guilty and to consider one's needs to be as important as those of others.

"Women, children, and members of ethnic minorities in the United States have characteristically been taught that assertive behavior is the province of the white, adult male. Indeed, such attitudes run deep and die hard in our culture."
Robert E. Alberti and Michael L. Emmons
Your Perfect Right, Impact 1974, page 4

exercise twenty-five: *45 minutes*

25   *"As a Women, I can't . . . ."**

Purpose: To help you change your view of what is possible for
women to do.

We often learn to behave according to what other people expect
of us as women, wives, mothers, workers, students, daughters,
etc. — and feel we cannot change.

Discussion: Can you think of a situation or event in which you
could not participate because you were a woman or in which
you felt it was not proper for a woman to act a certain way?
What held you back?

Procedure:

1. The group divides into pairs and each person, in turn,
   completes the following phrase to her partner —

   "As a woman, I can't _____."

   The partner listens and before replying with her own
   sentence, summarizes what the other has said to show
   that she heard.

2. Each pair then completes the phrase below and follows
   the same procedure.

   "As a woman, I don't choose to _____."

3. Using the same procedure, the pair completes the final
   phrase.

   "As a woman, I may be able to _____."

Discussion: In groups of six or eight, share what each felt they
could not do. Did changing the sentence change the feeling
about the difficulty of doing whatever it was? Are you willing
to try now? Tell others in the group how and when you will
try. How has your view of society's expectations limited your
activities?

----

*Contributed by Sherri Davidson, graduate student at Western Michigan University.

To the Leader:

If there are men in the group, you may substitute —
"As a man, I can't _____." See if men feel limited
by physical barriers (money, size, etc.), women by
psychological, social or legal barriers. Point out the
differences caused by culture and training.

This can also be used as an exercise in listening. The
discussion following could include — How difficult it is
to listen without thinking of a response before the other
person has finished. What has been your experience with
another person when you spoke and were not understood
or when you didn't listen?

exercise twenty-six: *30 minutes*

"Oh, You're One of Those Women Libbers!" *   **26**

Purpose: To help you learn how to react appropriately to sexist
comments.

Women frequently state that they feel inadequate to cope with
sexist "put-downs". The following exercise is an attempt to
help women gain some experience and learn some answers in
a supportive setting.

Discussion: What happens when someone makes a sexist remark
to you? How do you respond? How do you feel?

Procedure:

1. Participants divide into two groups.

2. One group will make a commonly used sexist statement
   and keep defending the statement with other sexist remarks.

3. The other group tries to think of appropriate responses
   which explain their feelings and are not defensive.

4. Groups then switch sides to state and reply to the same
   sexist statements.

---
*Contributed by June Mochizuki, Assistant Professor, Counseling Center, Western Michigan University.

Examples of sexist statements —

Why do you want to be called chairperson? There's no
such word. It's awkward.

Women are too emotional to be President.

Women make terrible bosses.

Women aren't strong enough to play on men's
athletic teams.

Oh, you're one of those women libbers!

You're a typical woman driver!

That's just like a woman!

Discussion: What feelings did you experience in defending your
side? What types of answers seemed to be most effective?   Why?

exercise twenty-seven: *2 hours*

27   *Building A Belief System*

Purpose: To help you develop a reliable rationale for acting
assertively.

A major goal of assertiveness training is to build a personal
belief system which will help a person support and justify
acting assertively. As Jakubowski-Spector states, this is
important so that a woman —

"1. Can continue to believe in her right to act assertively,
even if she is unjustly criticized.

2. Can counteract her own irrational guilt that may occur
later.

3. Can be proud of her assertion even if no one else is
pleased with the behavior.

4. Can be more likely to assert herself again. "*

---

*For a more detailed discussion of assertiveness training, see Patricia Jakubowski-Spector, *An Introduction to
Assertiveness Training Procedures for Women* (Washington, D. C.: American Personnel and Guidance
Association, 1973).

Basically, this belief system states that all persons have a right to their feelings, beliefs or opinions. Another person may not like your feelings but that doesn't detract from the legitimacy of them. Acting in an appropriate assertive way increases self-respect.

Discussion: Leader gives examples of aggressive behavior, assertive behavior, non-assertive behavior and non-assertive aggressive behavior. Read the definitions on pages 88-89 and then discuss the differences. Are the distinctions clear? Are there any points of discomfort?

Procedure:

1. Learning to distinguish between the different types of behavior.

   a. Leader asks a participant to volunteer telling about a situation in which she inhibited her honest, spontaneous reactions and ended feeling hurt, anxious or angry as a result. For example, saying "Sure, I'll be glad to baby-sit for you," when, in fact, she hates it.

   b. Leader asks for examples of aggressive behavior.

   c. Leader asks for examples of non-assertive aggressive behavior.

   d. Leader asks for examples of assertive behavior.

   To the Leader:

   It might be more interesting to demonstrate each type of behavior by having a couple of participants or leaders act out examples of the different behaviors.

2. Identifying personal non-assertive behavior and the feelings generated.

   a. Do the Assertiveness Inventory (page 92).

   b. Discuss the items in which there are discrepancies of two or more between degree of discomfort and probable response.

   c. Place a circle around the item number to indicate the situations you would like to handle more assertively.

3. Identifying your rights and/or irrational beliefs.

   a. Read the statement of Human Rights, page 94.
Do you agree? Are there more rights that should
be included in this declaration?

   b. In your support group, go over the Assertiveness
Inventory again and identify which of the Human Rights
were used in each situation.

   c. Analyze the Irrational Beliefs, page 95.

4. Analyzing the situation to uncover blocks to assertiveness.

   a. Using the Assertiveness Inventory, choose the circled
item or another situation in which you generally react
non-assertively.

   b. Each person in the group takes turns playing the
following roles —

Presenter: Briefly describes the actual situation.

Listener: Asks the four discussion questions below,
listens to Presenter and reflects the
content and underlying feelings which
the Presenter expresses.

Questions:

   1.   What were your feelings afterward?

   2.   What rights did you give up?

   3.   What do you wish you had said?

   4.   What made it hard or impossible for you
to say it?

Observers (remainder of group):   Carefully note the
interaction between Presenter and Listener. Make
suggestions when communication is blocked. Help
identify basic human rights or irrational beliefs.
At end of discussion, give feedback on what they
have observed.

Discussion: Group discusses why participants could not say "no"
or act assertively. What happens to a relationship if you don't
express your needs? What would happen if you said "no"? Is
it right to feel that you don't want to do certain things? How
important is it to you to act assertively? When?

The next exercise will help challenge your irrational thoughts.

To the Leader:

This procedure may take two or more sessions. Everyone should get a chance to re-enact an experience. Time should be set aside at the next session to discuss any experiences participants may have had on the outside.

The basis of many anxieties impeding assertive behavior may be irrational beliefs. These are revealed when the participant responds to the question, "What made it hard or impossible for you to say it?" Usually the irrational belief is something like, "Wouldn't it be awful if the other person's feelings got hurt. She/he would be permanently damaged and I would be totally responsible." Using Ellis' techniques, these thoughts can be replaced by rational thoughts. *

---

*Albert Ellis, *Reason and Emotion in Psychotherapy* (New York: Lyle Stuart, 1962).

Non-Assertive, Assertive, Aggressive and Non-Assertive Aggressive Behavior

Non-Assertive Behavior — is failing to stand up for yourself so that your rights are violated by another person. This occurs in either of two ways: First, you fail to assert yourself when someone takes advantage of you; second, failing to state your needs and feelings can result in an unintentional violation.

Often, non-assertive behavior is a subtle type of manipulation in which you renounce your rights in order to elicit a desired response from another person. For example:

Non-Assertive Behavior (The Unspoken Bargain)*

I won't assert myself when you —

(Boyfriend) ... constantly talk about your past girlfriends, socialize only with your friends, ridicule my opinions.

In exchange for your —

dating only me, changing these objectionable behaviors without my having to ask you to.

---

*Patricia Jakubowski-Spector, "Facilitating the Growth of Women Through Assertive Training" in *Counseling Psychologist*, Vol. 4, No. 1, 1973. p. 76.

(Husband) ... make me the scape-
   goat for your business
   frustrations, give me the
   "silent" treatment, are
   abrupt in sex.

staying married to me and
maintaining our home.

(Employer) ... frequently ask me
   to work during my lunch
   hour for no extra pay, un-
   fairly criticize me.

giving me a raise without my
having to ask for it, never
firing me.

* * * * *

<u>Assertive Behavior</u> — is standing up for your rights in a way that
   shows you also respect the rights of others. It is an honest,
   direct and appropriate expression of your feelings and opinions.
   It communicates respect rather than submission. It is focussed
   on behavior rather than criticism of the person.

<u>Aggressive Behavior</u> — is standing up for your rights in a way that
   humiliates, browbeats or degrades another person. It is
   frequently an over-reaction resulting from pent-up anger.
   Expressing your angry feelings when they occur is assertive.
   Holding other people responsible for your anger or humiliating
   them because you feel angry is aggressive behavior. Sarcasm
   is aggressive.

<u>Non-Assertive Aggressive (NAG) Behavior</u> — is failing to stand up
   for yourself in such a way so that the other person may feel
   humiliated, guilty or punished. Powerless groups, like women
   and minorities, often resort to this behavior. Examples are —
   accepting invitations but leaving early because of headaches,
   taking longer and doing a sloppy job on work assignments, sub-
   mitting but not responding in sexual intercourse. By agreeing
   to demands, but expressing aggression in an indirect way, you
   may escape blame or retaliation in the short run, but eventually
   the very relationship you are trying to protect deteriorates.

A Comparison of Non-Assertive, Assertive, Aggressive, Non-Assertive Agressive Behavior*

	Non-Assertive Behavior	Assertive Behavior	Aggressive Behavior	(NAG) Non-Assertive Aggressive Behavior
Characteristics of the behavior	Emotionally dishonest, indirect, self-denying, Allows others to choose for her. Does not achieve desired goal.	Emotionally honest, direct, self-enhancing, expressive. Chooses for self. May achieve goal.	Emotionally honest, direct, self-enhancing at the expense of another, expressive. Chooses for others. May achieve goal at expense of others.	Emotionally dishonest, indirect, self-denying. Chooses for others. May achieve goal at expense of others.
Your feelings	Hurt, anxious, possibly angry later.	Confident, self-respecting.	Righteous, superior, derogative at the time and possibly guilty later.	Defiance, anger, self-denying. Sometimes anxious, possibly guilty later.
The other person's feelings toward you	Irritated, pity, lack of respect.	Generally respect	Angry, resentful	Angry, resentful, irritated, disgusted.
The other person's feelings about her/himself	Guilty or superior.	Valued, respected.	Hurt, embarrassed, defensive.	Hurt, guilty or superior, humiliated.

*Idea from Robert E. Alberti and Michael Emmons, *Your Perfect Right: A Guide to Assertive Behavior* (San Luis Obispo, Calif.: Impact, 1970). p. 11.

Assertiveness Inventory*

Many people feel varying degrees of discomfort in handling interpersonal situations requiring them to assert themselves in some way.

Please indicate your degree of discomfort in the space provided before each situation below. Use the following scale to indicate degree of discomfort. For example, if you feel a little discomfort when complimenting a friend, mark "2" in the space before the situation described.

Discomfort Scale:

        1 = none

        2 = a little

        3 = a fair amount

        4 = much

        5 = very much

Then go over the list a second time and indicate after each item the probability or chance of your displaying the behavior in a situation. For example, if you rarely apologize when you are at fault, you would mark a "4" after that item. Use the following scale to indicate response probability.

Response Probability:

        1 = always do it

        2 = usually do it

        3 = do it about half the time

        4 = rarely do it

        5 = never do it

---

*Modified from Elaine D. Gambrill and C. A. Richey, "An Assertion Inventory for Use in Assessment and Research" (in *Behavior Therapy*, Vol. 6, 1975). p. 550-56.

Degree of Discomfort	Situation	Response Probability
....	1. Refusing a request to borrow something you value (homework, car, money, etc.)	....
....	2. Complimenting a friend	....
....	3. Asking a favor of someone	....
....	4. Resisting sales pressure	....
....	5. Apologizing when you are at fault	....
....	6. Refusing a request for a meeting or date	....
....	7. Admitting fear and requesting consideration	
....	8. Telling a person who is very close to you that something he/she says or does bothers you	....
....	9. Asking for a raise	....
....	10. Turning off a talkative friend	
....	11. Requesting a date with a person	....
....	12. Admitting confusion about a point under discussion and asking for clarification	....
....	13. Applying for a job	....
....	14. Requesting expected service when it is not forthcoming e.g., in a restaurant, store, etc.	....
....	15. Discussing openly with a person his/her criticism of your behavior	....
....	16. Returning defective items to a store	....
....	17. Expressing an opinion that differs from that of the person you are talking to	....
....	18. Resisting sexual overtures when you are not interested	....
....	19. Telling someone good news about yourself	....
....	20. Resisting pressure to drink or smoke pot	....
....	21. Quitting a job	
....	22. Discussing openly with a person his/her criticism of your work	
....	23. Requesting the return of borrowed items	....
....	24. Receiving compliments	....
....	25. Continuing to converse with someone who disagrees	

As a final step, indicate the situations you would like to handle more assertively by circling the item number.

Human Rights

. . . **Right** to refuse requests without having to feel guilty or selfish.

. . . **Right** to feel and express feelings including anger, as long as we don't violate the rights of others.

. . . **Right** to be competitive and to achieve.

. . . **Right** to enjoy rest and leisure.

. . . **Right** to have one's needs be as important as the needs of other people.

. . . **Right** to decide which activities will fulfill those needs.

. . . **Right** to make mistakes.

. . . **Right** to have one's opinions given the same respect and consideration that other people's opinions are given.

. . . **Right** to be treated as a capable adult and taken seriously.

. . . **Right** to be independent.

. . . **Right** to get what we pay for.

. . . **Right** to ask for information from professionals.

. . . **Right** to decide when to be assertive.

Rights Also Involve Responsibilities

exercise twenty-eight:

Analysis of Irrational Beliefs   **28**

Purpose: To learn how to replace irrational beliefs with rational thoughts.

Many times, powerful, irrational and illogical ideas stand in the way of our leading anxiety-free, nonhostile, assertive lives. We tend to take these ideas and carry them to extremes — "awfulizing" according to Albert Ellis.

In order to act assertively, we must replace these irrational thoughts with rational ones which permit us to act. Below are some of the most common Irrational Beliefs taken from a list by Ellis. *

Procedure: Read the following Irrational Ideas and Awfulizing Thoughts and then write some of your own in the space given.

Irrational Idea: It is a dire necessity for an adult to be loved or approved by almost everyone for virtually everything he/she does.

Awfulizing Thought: If I say or do this, people won't like me, nobody will like me, I will be alone forever.

Irrational Idea: One should be thoroughly competent, adequate, and achieving in all possible respects.

Awfulizing Thought: If I make a mistake or don't do this perfectly, I'm no good.

Irrational Idea: Human unhappiness is externally caused and people have little or no ability to control their sorrows or rid themselves of their negative feelings.

Awfulizing Thought: Therefore, I must never say or do anything to hurt anybody because the person will be permanently damaged and I would be totally responsible.

---

*From Albert Ellis and Robert A. Harper, *A Guide to Rational Living* (North Hollywood, Calif., Wilshire Book Co., 1970).

You may have other irrational beliefs in which you "awfulize"
and situations in which you did not act assertively. What
"self-talk" did you use?

....

....

....

How did you awfulize?

....

....

Discussion: Share with your group your "self-talk" and how you
"awfulized." Ask the group to help you discover why your
"self-talk" is irrational. Review again the statement of
Human Rights, page 94.

exercise twenty-nine:

29   *Counteracting Irrational Thoughts*

Purpose: To develop a technique for coping with irrational thoughts.

The best way to prepare yourself for a situation which is
threatening is to list on paper the "self-talk" which creates
your feelings of anxiety or anger. The next step is to challenge
or counteract each statement.

Procedure: Think of a situation you will be facing in the near
future in which you would like to act assertively but you feel
handicapped by either anxiety or anger.

1. Write a brief description of the situation and your feelings.

....

....

....

2. In the column on the left, list the thoughts that pass quickly
   through your mind which cause you to become anxious or
   angry when you think about acting assertively during your
   situation. Next, think about what makes that thought so awful
   and write that down in the same column.

For example:

1. If I tell John I don't want to date him, I will hurt his feelings.

2. He will feel terribly, terribly hurt.

3. It will be all my fault.

Self-talk that produces negative feelings	Counteracting statements
1.	1.
2.	2.
3.	3.
4.	4.
5.	5.

3. Now go back and challenge each item of self-talk. Write your challenges in the right column above. To challenge each statement, look at it logically and rationally. Besides your self-talk, there are at least three other ways to look at the same statement:

1. There is just as much chance the opposite will happen.

2. It may affect some people one way, an equal number the other way.

3. If it did happen, does it matter? Can you handle it? Can the other people involved handle it?

   In addition, do you have alternative ways of responding to the same situation? Does it really mean you are no good, unlovable, stupid, will always be alone, etc. ?

4. Also, consider your Human Rights.

5. Write your challenges in the form of a different kind of self-talk that you could use instead of the negative self-talk expressed in the first column.

Discussion: Did this exercise help you with your anxious or angry feelings about the situation you will be facing? How? If you still feel anxious or angry, the exercises in behavior rehearsal will help.

exercise thirty: *2 hours*

30   *Behavior Rehearsal and Escalation*

Purpose: To add assertive skills to your behavior repertoire
and reduce anxiety about acting assertively.

Behavior rehearsal can be quite useful in reducing your
anxiety about asserting yourself in two ways:

1. As you perceive your increased skill in handling
   successively difficult role-playing experiences
   your self-confidence will increase.

2. You will learn through the course of role-playing
   that nothing catastrophic happens when you act
   assertively.

Discussion: Review the differences between assertive, non-
assertive, aggressive and non-assertive aggressive behavior.
Reread the basic Human Rights. Then discuss with your
leader and the other participants any questions or conflicts
you may have. Are there any of the rights you question?
Are there more you can add? (Different situations will
involve different rights.)

Procedure: Divide into groups of six. Each member of the
support group in turn follows the procedure below:

1. Think of a situation which has happened or will happen
   in which you would like to act assertively. Explain it
   briefly to the group.

2. Act out the situation to the person on your right. Say
   what you would like to say or wished you had said. She
   is to listen only.

3. The rest of the group gives feedback on what made your
   actions or words non-assertive (or assertive or aggressive,
   etc.) using the Assertiveness Training Checklist, page 100.

4. The group asks "why" it is hard to be assertive in the
   situation you described to expose any irrational thinking.

5. Re-enact the same situation with the second person on your right. She responds by giving you a mild hassle. You try to respond to the hassle assertively.

6. The group provides feedback on anything that may detract from assertive behavior. (Refer to the checklist again.)

7. Re-enact the situation with a third person who responds with a medium hassle.

8. Group again gives feedback.

9. Re-enact the situation with a fourth person who responds with a big hassle.

10. Group gives feedback.

11. The fifth person acts as an observer and sees that the group stays with the procedures as outlined above.

Discussion: Were you pleased with your performance? Any comments or reactions to the process? Do you feel you can act this way on the outside now?

Pick a situation with a roommate or friend in which you will try to act more assertively. Decide on the time and place with your group and report back the results later.

To the Leader:

The two parts of this exercise may take two, three or four sessions to complete depending on how deep the group wishes to go. Some members may need no more than an introduction to the concepts and a brief rehearsal. With others, the group and leaders will need to spend more time developing a belief system, motivation, and working on irrational fears.

Bibliography

For more detailed discussions of assertiveness training, see the following:

Alberti, Robert E., and Emmons, Michael L., *Stand Up, Speak Out, Talk Back*. New York: Pocket Books, 1975.

Bloom, Lynn Z., Coburn, Karen, and Pearlman, Joan, *The New Assertive Woman*. New York: Dell Book, 1976.

Fensterheim, Herbert, and Baer, Jean, *Don't Say Yes When You Want To Say No*. New York: David McKay Co., 1975.

Jakubowski-Spector, Patricia, *An Introduction to Assertive Training Procedures for Women*. Washington, D.C.: American Personnel and Guidance Association, 1973.

Lange, Arthur J., and Jakubowski, Patricia, *Responsible Assertive Behavior*. Champaign, Ill.: Research Press, 1976.

Phelps, Stanlee, and Austin, Nancy, *The Assertive Woman*. San Luis Obispo, Calif.: Impact, 1975.

Smith, Manuel J., *When I Say No, I Feel Guilty*. New York: Bantam Books, 1975.

Assertiveness Training Checklist

1.   How did you look?

     Eye contact ?

     Relaxed posture?

     Nervous laughing or joking?

     Excessive or unrelated hand and body movements?

2.   What did you say?

     Comments concise, to the point, appropriately assertive to the situation?

     Comments definite and firm?

     A factual statement with no long-winded explanations, excuses or apologetic behavior?

3.   How did you say it?

     An immediate response to what the other person said?

     No whining, pleading, sarcasm?

4.   How did you feel about your performance?

     Did you gain in self-respect?

     Rate yourself on your SUDS (Subjective Units of Disturbance) score below:

0   100
Relaxed   Panic Stricken

IX. Improving Communication in Interpersonal Relationships

Using listening and feedback techniques, conflict resolution and expressing
feelings constructively. See also: Leadership Training
        Speaking and Listening
        How To Give and Receive Feedback
        Adverse Feedback
        Conflict Resolution

"Things are seldom what they seem,
skim milk masquerades as cream.
Externals don't portray insides,
Jekylls may be masking Hydes."
        Sidney M. Jourard *(The Transparent Self.*
        Van Nostrand Reinhold Company, N.Y.
        1971, p. 4)

exercise thirty-one: *60 minutes*

31   *Speaking and Listening*

Purpose: To improve the quality of our listening and speaking
as an aid to better personal relationships.

Our effectiveness in our relations with others — whether friends,
family or people in authority — depends to a great extent on the
quality of our speaking and listening. We are often so busy
preparing a reply that we do not hear what is really said. The
other person feels frustrated at not being able to get a message
across. Both speaking and listening place certain responsibilities
on us. We can improve both our listening and our speaking by
practicing certain skills described in this exercise.

Discussion: Can you remember an experience when you spoke to
a group or to an individual and could not seem to make yourself
understood? How did you feel? Can you remember an experience
when you found you were not being listened to? How did you feel?

Procedure:

1. Read the following to become aware of what actually occurs
   during an interaction between two people. *

   (a) A speaker may be uncertain what she wishes to say. The
   message may be jumbled or consist of conflicting thoughts.
   There is a tendency for listeners to judge an unclear
   message as either positive or negative based on past experience with the speaker.

   (b) A listener may stop listening because she thinks she
   already knows what the speaker is going to say before
   the speaker has finished her statement.

   (c) A listener often hears the beginning and end of a statement but little of what is said in the middle.

   (d) A listener tends to ignore ideas that she disagrees with
   or does not understand.

_____

*From D. T. Campbell, "Systematic Error on the Part of Human Links in Communications Systems" as quoted
from "Information and Control" by Gerard Egan (chapter 7 in *Encounter: Group Processes for Interpersonal
Growth,* Belmont, Calif.: Brooks-Cole Publishing Co., 1970) pp. 254-258.

(e) When two people are interacting in the listening and speaking process, there are times when the speaker and listener get confused ideas about what one is <u>saying</u> and the other is <u>hearing</u>.

2. Now read: RESPONSIBILITIES OF THE SPEAKER*

(a) Try to organize your thoughts before deciding to speak.

(b) Ask the listener to help you clarify your ideas if your thoughts are coming out jumbled. "What am I trying to say?"

(c) Use brief statements.

(d) Check to see if the listener understands what you are saying. "Am I being clear?"

(e) Check to see if the listener is involved. "Are you following me?"

(f) If you are interrupted by the listener, you may ask the listener to wait until you are finished. "This idea may be different from what I have said before. Wait until I finish."

(g) When asking questions, be sure to get answers that relate directly to your questions as opposed to answers which are irrelevant.

3. Here are: RESPONSIBILITIES OF THE LISTENER

(a) If you choose to listen, then listen and look attentive. Look at and face the speaker while he or she is talking.

(b) Make a special effort to keep with the speaker if her remarks are lengthy.

(c) If the speaker talks at length, intervene occasionally to remain involved. "Are you saying . . . ?"

(d) Ask for clarification when you are confused. "I'm confused about that last point."

(e) Respond with nods, "Yes" and "Um hmm" to encourage people to continue and to indicate understanding.

(f) <u>Concentrate on listening</u> — <u>don't reply until the speaker is finished</u>.

(g) Whenever appropriate, summarize what you believe is the content of the speaker's message to check your understanding of what is being said.

*Adapted from Margaret J. Freeman and Lee E. Pelton, *Learning Skills of Interaction — A Group Approach* (Detroit, Mich.: Harlo Press, 1972) pp. 71-73.

4. Now form into groups of three: a listener, a speaker and an observer.

   The speaker selects topics from the list below to discuss for five minutes:

   - It's OK for men to tell dirty jokes but it's not ladylike for women.

   - Women earning as much as their dates do should bear the expense equally when they go out together.

   - Married women with pre-school children should not work outside the home.

   - Intoxication among women is worse than intoxication among men.

   - To best serve the needs of the city, the position of Chief of Police should be filled by a man.

5. Ground Rule: Each listener is to summarize in her own words what she believes the speaker said and verify her understanding with the speaker <u>before</u> giving her own ideas.

6. The observer helps reinforce the rule by stopping the communication process at an appropriate time to check whether or not both listener and speaker agree that they are using the ground rule to one another's satisfaction.

7. At the end of five minutes, the observer gives feedback to the speaker and listener using the following guidelines:

Observer's Guidelines

Does the Speaker —

(a) Sound as though she has organized her thoughts before speaking?

(b) Ask the listener to help her clarify her thoughts about what she is trying to say?

(c) Use brief statements?

(d) Check to see if the listener understands what is being said?

(e) Ask the listener to wait until she is finished speaking when she is interrupted?

(f) Continue talking when she is asked a question before giving an answer?

(g) Keep rephrasing a question thereby confusing or complicating the original question?

Does the Listener —

(a) Appear attentive through both facial expression and body language?

(b) Make a special effort by intervening or concentrating on listening when the speaker's remarks are lengthy?

(c) Ask for clarification when she is confused?

(d) Sum up what she believes the speaker is saying?

(Note to Observer: Notice anything else about either the speaker or listener that either impedes or helps the interaction.)

8. After the Observer gives her report, the three participants may want to discuss the exchange briefly.

9. Members change roles until each has experienced each role.

Discussion: In the larger group, discuss — What seemed to be the behavior that most interfered with developing the topic discussed? Did having to summarize before responding affect the Listener in any way? Speaker?

To the Leader:

You may want to demonstrate each of the roles at the start in order to clarify the exercise.

exercise thirty-two: *60 minutes*

How To Give and Receive Feedback   **32**

Purpose: To learn the skills of giving and receiving feedback.

Feedback is communicating information to a person or group about how that person or group appears or affects other people. Feedback gives the person a chance to see if her behavior matches her intentions. It is a way of learning "Who am I?" and helping to consider whether or not to change behavior. Feedback is necessary in many kinds of relationships — familial, social, supervisory. Feedback helps maintain the relationship, insure closeness and increase awareness of self and one's effect on another person's behavior.

Feedback can be destructive rather than constructive if it is not done properly. The following exercise will help you learn the skills of giving and receiving feedback effectively.

Discussion: Can you remember a time when someone — a friend, teacher or supervisor — told you something about yourself that you were not aware of? What were your feelings when you were told? How do you feel about it now?

Procedure: The following criteria should be observed to make sure that feedback is constructive —

Criteria for Constructive Feedback*

Constructive Feedback —

(a) Describes rather than judges. It describes both the action and the feeling the action arouses. Describing your own reaction leaves the person free to use the feedback or not, or to use it as he or she sees fit.

"When you do this, I feel . . . ."

(b) Is specific rather than general. To be told that you are "domineering" or "lazy" or "insensitive" is not as useful as to be told, "When we were deciding that issue, it seemed to me that you did not listen to the others. I felt I had to decide between accepting your point of view or being attacked by you."

Or, "When you leave a mess in the kitchen everytime you eat, I get angry because I feel you expect me to clean up after you since I hate messy kitchens."

(c) Is directed toward behavior the receiver can do something about. Self-concepts suffer and frustration increases when a person is reminded of something over which he can do nothing. Comments such as, "Wow, are you tall!" for example.

(d) Is asked for rather than imposed. Generally, feedback is apt to be more usefully received when the person has asked in some way for reactions to his or her behavior.

(e) Is given as soon after the action as possible, depending on whether the person is ready to hear feedback.

---

*Modified from "Feedback and the Helping Relationship," in NTL *Reading Book in Human Relations Training* (Washington, D.C.: NTL for Applied Behavioral Science, NEA, circa 1967). pp. 4-5.

(f) Is <u>tentative</u> rather than certain. After all, you are not a mind reader. You can only go by your perceptions of another's behavior. Another person may perceive it differently.

"You seemed angry when you ..."

(g) Is <u>checked</u> to be sure the listener hears and understands. One way to do this is to ask the listener to summarize the feedback to see if what the listener has heard corresponds with what the speaker had in mind.

Now do the following exercises for a newly formed group.

1. Divide into groups of three — a listener, a speaker and an observer. Pick persons for your triad you do not know or do not know well.

2. The speaker talks about herself for five minutes, telling about her family, home, goals and interests.

3. The listener responds by telling the speaker what she has perceived about the speaker not only from her words but from her appearance, manner and behavior. She may even comment on the speaker's personality, character, likes and dislikes. The speaker listens to the feedback <u>without responding</u>.

4. The observer gives feedback to the listener using the Criteria for Constructive Feedback as a guide.

5. The speaker can respond to the feedback as to accuracy (see "g" in the Criteria) and tells her reactions. The observer can also give her impressions now in order to verify or disagree with the accuracy of the feedback. An important question is, "Is this one person's impression or is the impression shared by others?" Impressions shared by others are less apt to be the result of stereotyping and bias.

Discussion: In large group or in support groups of six, discuss — Was the feedback accurate? How did you feel receiving it? How did you feel giving it?

You, yourself, are the only judge as to the accuracy of the feedback. It is up to you to accept or reject. One way of testing the accuracy is to see if the others in the group see you the same way. You may want to do that now. If there is a difference in how you see yourself and how others see you, you might comment or ask the others for help to identify the mixed signals you are sending.

exercise thirty-three: *60 minutes*

33   *Adverse Feedback**
*(To be done in a group that has already established trust
and acceptance.)*

Purpose: To learn how to handle adverse feedback.

Procedure:

1. Divide into groups of six to ten. Write down the first names of all the members in the group, proceeding clockwise from the leader. Leave a space between each name.

2. Place asterisks next to the names of members for whom you have the most positive feelings.

3. Now each of you in turn tell the individuals whose names you indicated with an asterisk why you feel that way about them. You must look directly at the person to whom you are speaking. Use the Criteria for Constructive Feedback, page 106.

4. Using the same list, write a short piece of adverse feedback, not to exceed 15 words, about each participant. Your comments will be presented in such a way as to be anonymous. (You have about 10-15 minutes.) Use the Criteria for Constructive Feedback.

5. Rearrange your chairs so that your group is seated in a semi-circle with one empty chair facing the semi-circle.

6. Hand your papers face down to a member of the group selected to read the papers. This person sits behind the semi-circle.

7. Each participant in turn, including the leader, sits in the feedback chair.

8. There are three phases for receiving feedback, as follows:

   (a) Anticipate aloud what adverse feedback you expect from the group.

   (b) The processor will read the comments written about you. You may respond to any extent you feel appropriate.

---
*Adapted from J. William Pfeiffer and John E. Jones, *A Handbook of Structured Experiences for Human Relations Training,* Vol. 1 (Iowa City, Iowa: University Associates Press, 1970). pp. 82-84.

(c) Comment on the degree of agreement between your own anticipation and the group's perceptions as shown by their feedback. If you are perceived differently by different members of the group, you may want to comment on possible explanations.

9. The group in the semi-circle does not comment or react to the person receiving feedback at this time to prevent an overload of feedback.

Discussion: After everyone has had a turn receiving feedback, discuss in your group how you felt. If you don't understand why you received some feedback, you may ask what behavior of yours generated that particular reaction. Continue this until every member of the group understands which specific behavior or signal provokes certain general reactions.

To the Leader:

If one member has a reaction to the receiver that is different from all the other members, the reasons for this may be worth pursuing. Usually that member is not "seeing" the receiver but is reacting to her feelings about someone the receiver reminds her of (herself, friend, relative, etc.)

exercise thirty-four: *60 minutes*

Conflict Resolution   34
"Have A Good Fight"

Purpose: To make you aware of how you handle conflicts and help develop more satisfactory ways of coping with irritations.

It is almost impossible for two or more people to live or work together for any length of time without some irritation or conflict. Most people try to ignore the irritating behavior, but the resulting feelings accumulate and become a barrier to maintaining the relationship and, often, to the accomplishment of the group in a work situation. Sometimes a person can store up so many feelings against another that he or she finally explodes out of all proportion to the trifling incident that triggered the explosion. Others may resolve their anger by withdrawing. Neither response is productive or satisfying.

The first exercise in this section will help to make you aware of your own style of handling conflict; the second helps you to practice a more desirable way.

Discussion: How do you handle conflicts in your personal relationships? Are you satisfied? How do you handle conflicts in a group situation? Are you satisfied?

Procedure:

1. Pick a partner. Face each other in a sitting position with knees touching and eyes closed. Join hands. (This is a non-verbal exercise, done without speaking.)

2. Leader reads aloud:

    Pretend you are greeting your partner, whom you have known well, on the street after a long absence. Show how you feel about seeing her again. Since your eyes are closed and you may not speak, you must communicate using only pressure from hands and knees.

3. Leader reads aloud:

    You have a nice conversation with your friend and catch up with each other's activities. However, you soon find yourselves in violent disagreement. You both become extremely angry with each other. Communicate your anger non-verbally. (Allow five minutes)

4. Leader reads aloud:

    You settle your argument and make up. Show how you do this non-verbally.

5. Leader reads:

    Now you must part. You are not sure when you will see each other again. Say goodbye to each other non-verbally.

Discussion: How did you act during the argument? Who started first? Were you passive? Active? Did you give up? Fight to the finish? Do you behave this same way in real life conflict situations?

To the Leader:

    If the leader or the group wishes, each part of this exercise can be discussed to clarify typical behavior for greetings, apologies and farewells.

Have a "Good" Fight Exercise

Procedure:

1. Look around your support group and pick a person with whom you feel especially comfortable. Go sit beside her.

2. When everyone has made a selection, take turns telling the chosen person why you feel comfortable with her. (There may be clusters of more than two people as the selection process will not automatically produce a pairing by twos and may result in several members of the group selecting the same "comfortable" person.)

3. Look around your support group again and pick another person toward whom you have uncomfortable feelings. Go sit beside her. (Again, there may be clusters.)

4. Take turns describing your uncomfortable feelings. Try to discover the reasons. Are there mannerisms that annoy you? Does the person remind you of someone else? Yourself, perhaps? A part of yourself you do not like? A specific behavior? Are you competing?

   Remember to use the Criteria for Constructive Feedback.

   Keep up the discussion of uncomfortable feelings until you both feel that the barrier between you is gone. Usually the uncomfortable feelings are mutual. Ask the other person to tell you how she feels about you. Remember your uncomfortable feelings are your problem and your responsibility. Whether consciously or unconsciously, you made the decision to feel uncomfortable.

Discussion: In small support groups, discuss: What happened to the uncomfortable feelings when you talked about them and understood them? Did you pick someone or wait to be picked? Why? If you were picked, are there any new uncomfortable feelings? If so, you need to talk about them now with either the person involved or with the group. To resolve conflict, it is important to stay with the discussion until a mutually satisfying situation is reached. Can you act this way in the real world?

To the Leader:

   It may be necessary to leave time at the beginning of the next session to check for left-over or new uncomfortable feelings. Watch for personality clashes and stop the group to work out conflicts using the method in the exercise.

X. Leadership Training

Learning skills of decision making, group techniques, and discussion leading.

How to Lead A Group
What's My Behavior In A Task Group
Characteristics of a Good Group
Group Observation Check List
Group Decision Making

See also: Improving Communications
Decision Making

"Women in this country do not want to be free for ruthless competition . . . . They want a place in public life for the values they have been forced to cherish in private far too long."
Vivian Gornick and Barbara K. Moran
(Woman in Sexist Society, Signet N.Y. 1972
p. xxx)

exercise thirty-five:

How To Lead A Group   **35**

Purpose: To help you understand the basic qualities of group leadership.

Much of the work in our culture is accomplished through group decision and group effort. People work in committees, task forces, job groups and discussion groups. Being a member of a group and leading a group are both important skills and the skills are similar. This section will give you some information and describe how to get experience.

Discussion: How do you rate yourself as a group leader? As a group member? What is your biggest difficulty when you lead a group? When you are a group member?

Procedure: Please read the following —

1. Definition of a group. A group is a collection of people with a common goal who interact dynamically with each other. There is movement toward the goal and consent among the members to move in this direction. They have a capacity for self-direction.

2. The most effective groups, as proven by research —

    (a) Have stated goals agreed to by all members.

    (b) Are democratically run, recognizing that "All of us are smarter than any of us." Each person has some unique knowledge, attitude, skill or experience that others do not have.

    (c) Develop mutual feelings of trust and acceptance.

    (d) Accept and value members who are different.

    (e) Direct help toward the problems causing the group the most immediate concern.

    (f) Start with one person's perception of a problem.

    (g) Feel secure enough eventually so that the need to shut out unwanted information decreases.

3. The life cycle of a group passes through several phases:

    (a) Initial phase. Interaction is apt to be superficial, interchange is stilted and not spontaneous. Ideas or suggestions are not followed through and are usually left undeveloped. Individuals seem to hear and see relatively little of what is really going on.

    (b) Honeymoon phase. Feelings of warmth and support are generated. Most interaction is directed toward developing and maintaining these feelings.

    (c) Conflict and growth phase. Participants feel secure enough to work out interpersonal conflicts and test feelings about authority.

    (d) Mature phase. Members can now try out new behavior and get honest feedback.

    (e) Farewell or termination phase. Experience within the group is linked to related situations outside the group.

4. Roles of leaders and members:

    (a) Tasks or goals. In a democratically run group, the leader fosters a feeling of responsibility in the members to fulfill their tasks. The leader and each member have the responsibility for —

        (1) Initiating. Proposing tasks or goals; defining a group problem; suggesting a procedure or ideas for solving a problem.

        (2) Seeking information or opinions. Requesting facts; seeking relevant information about group concerns. Asking for expressions of feeling; requesting a statement or estimate; soliciting expressions of value or seeking suggestions and ideas.

        (3) Giving information or opinions. Offering facts; providing relevant information about group concern; stating a belief about a matter before the group; giving suggestions and ideas.

        (4) Clarifying and elaborating. Interpreting ideas or suggestions; clearing up confusions; defining terms; indicating alternatives and issues before the group.

(5) Summarizing. Pulling together related ideas; restating suggestions after the group has discussed them; offering a decision or conclusion for the group to accept or reject.

(6) Consensus testing. Asking to see if group is nearing a decision; sending up a trial balloon to test a possible conclusion.

(b) Group maintenance. The following are types of behavior needed to keep a group in good working order, maintaining a healthy climate for task work and good relationships which permit maximum use of member resources.

(1) Harmonizing. Attempting to reconcile disagreements, reducing tension, getting people to explore differences.

(2) Gate Keeping. Helping to keep communication channels open; facilitating the participation of others; suggesting procedures that permit sharing remarks.

(3) Encouraging. Being friendly, warm and responsive to others; indicating by facial expression or comment the acceptance of others' contributions.

(4) Compromising. When leader's own idea or status is involved in conflict, offering a compromise which yields status, admits error and modifies idea in the interest of group cohesion or growth.

(5) Standard setting and testing. Periodically testing whether group is satisfied with its procedures; suggesting other procedures; pointing out explicit norms which have been set to make them available for testing.

5. What all groups have in common:

(a) All participants need to feel secure before they can look, explore, feel free to express underlying basis for their actions.

(b) The group strives to cultivate an atmosphere in which a member continues to feel acceptance despite possible rejection of his or her idea.

(c) A group offers a place to test the reality of an idea and it is the role of the leader or other members to react honestly.

(d) Members present their feelings not only through the words they speak but also by body language, posture, gestures of hands and facial expression.

(e) The more members participate in a group, the more they get out of it.

(f) The group is strengthened by recognizing individual differences instead of merely focusing on points of similarity and consensus.

(g) People react according to their perceptions of a situation. Perceptions are usually based on past experience.

(h) Two levels of agendas are going on — Surface or Stated Agenda and Hidden Agenda or Feelings. *

> (1) Hidden agendas are all the different motives, desires, aspirations and emotional reactions held by the group members that cannot be fitted legitimately into the accepted group task. Hidden agendas can impede the progress of the group unless brought to the surface.

> (2) Hidden agendas are neither good nor bad but need to be recognized and worked on as much as the surface agenda.

> (3) There will be a lessening of feelings of guilt about hidden agendas and tendency to bring them to the surface if groups are aided in bringing conflicts out into the open. The leader might say, "We certainly must expect each of us to see things differently since that is all part of the differences that make up a group. I wonder if we have said all we feel about this. Let's go around the group and see if any more thoughts can be opened up."

> (4) When hidden agendas can be discussed, they are easier to handle. However, there are some hidden feelings which would hurt the group more if they were talked about openly. A leader needs to be sensitive enough to recognize what can and cannot be handled by the group.

> (5) Methods can be worked out by the group for solving hidden agendas. Problem solving can be used such as the technique described in the section on decision making.

6. Conclusion:

(a) In spite of all attempts at democratic leadership, the title or role of Leader does give weight to the leader's opinions, attitudes and decisions. A rule of thumb: When asking for opinions or decisions, express yours

---

*Leland P. Bradford, ''The Case of the Hidden Agenda'' in *Leaders Digest*, Vol. 1, 1953, pp. 36-46. (Washington, D.C.: NTL Institute)

last. When demonstrating an exercise or asking for an
expression of feeling, express yours first.

(b) Keep a flexible attitude and say so when necessary.
"I'm always learning. I'll do the best I can. If I do
anything wrong or you don't agree with me, let me
know."

Procedure: Each participant takes a turn leading a discussion of
any of the exercises in the manual and in conducting an exercise.

Discussion: During the last 15 minutes (before the session
evaluation), have the participants give feedback to the person
who was group leader as follows:

What did she do very well as group leader?

What does she need to work on?

References

Benne, K., & Sheats, P., "Functional Roles of Group Members." *Journal of Social
Issues,* Vol. 4, Spring, 1948. pp. 42-47.
Bradford, Leland P., "The Case of the Hidden Agenda." *Readers Digest,* No. 1, 1953.
Gazda, G. M., *Group Counseling: A Developmental Approach,* Boston: Allyn and
Bacon, 1971.
Kemp, C. Gratton, *Perspectives On the Group Process,* (2nd ed.) Boston: Houghton
Mifflin, 1970, Parts IV and V. "Leadership," pp. 153-240; "The Group Member,"
pp. 241-333.
Lieberman, Morton A., Yalom, Irwin D., and Miles, Matthew B., *Encounter Groups:
First Facts.* New York: Basic Books, 1973.
Lifton, Walter, *Groups: Facilitating Individual Growth and Societal Changes.* New
York: John Wiley & Sons, Inc., 1972.
Mills, Theodore, "Toward a Conception of the Life Cycle of Groups" in Theodore Mills
& Stan Rosenberg (Eds.), *Readings on the Sociology of Small Groups.* Englewood
Cliffs, New Jersey: Prentice Hall, 1970. pp. 238-247.

exercise thirty-six: *60 minutes*

36   *What's My Behavior in a Task Group?*
                                including
          "How Well Are Our Institutions Serving The Country?"
                                  and
                  "Characteristics of a Good Group"

Purpose: To learn the roles each participant plays in a group;
         to practice group procedures and analyze phases; and
         to practice giving feedback.

Procedure:

1. Divide into two groups of at least five persons each. One
   group will do the tasks and is placed in a circle and given
   worksheets for either the "How Well Are Our Institutions
   Serving the Country?" exercise or the "Characteristics
   of a Good Group" exercise.

2. The second group will act as observers and places itself
   around the outside of the task group and is given the
   "Group Observation Check List" to follow.

3. After the group doing the exercises reaches consensus,
   the leader can read the answers from the key.

4. Each person in the task group in turn responds to two
   questions:

   > What did I contribute as a member of the group?

   > What could I have done better?

5. In giving feedback, the observers are cautioned to use the
   Criteria for Constructive Feedback on page 106. They are
   giving their perceptions and should phrase their feedback
   so that it is tentative, non-judgmental and specific. They
   must check to see if their perceptions were accurate.

6. When the discussion is completed, the groups change places
   and do a consensus-reaching task. (This can be done at
   another session, if time is running short.)

Discussion: Does your perception of your role agree with the
observers? Can you explain any discrepancies? Was the
feedback given correctly? Were you made to feel defensive
at any time? Do you behave or play the same role in other
group situations?

"How Well Are Our Institutions Serving the Country?"
Worksheet

1. You are being interviewed by a survey team from the University of Michigan Institute for Social Research. You are asked to rank order the institutions listed below according to how well these institutions serve the country, in your opinion. On the left side of the page place a number "1" beside the institution you believe is serving the country best, a number "2" next to the second best and so on through number "15" — the institution serving the country least. Do not discuss your choice with the others in your task group. You will have 10 minutes.

Your Rank	Institution	Group Rank
_____	Federal Government	_____
_____	Colleges and Universities	_____
_____	U. S. Military	_____
_____	President and Administration	_____
_____	Labor Unions	_____
_____	Churches and Religious Organizations	_____
_____	Local Governments	_____
_____	Judicial System — All Courts except Supreme	_____
_____	Public Schools	_____
_____	Small Businesses	_____
_____	U. S. Congress	_____
_____	State Governments	_____
_____	Large Corporations	_____
_____	News Media	_____
_____	U. S. Supreme Court	_____

2. Now, as a group, you must agree through consensus which of the institutions should be ranked "1" through "15". Do not vote. Consensus means an agreement reached at least in part by every member of the group. List the group decision on the right. You will have 30 minutes.

To the Leader:

> Another use for this exercise is in the valuing section.
> This exercise involves societal values and the partici-
> pants' willingness to defend their values publicly. If
> used for a values assignment, the discussion can center
> on the following questions: How did you feel defending
> your choices? What did you think the others felt about
> your choices? What values were you defending? Why
> did you relinquish some?

"How Well Are Our Institutions Serving The Country?"

KEY

The following rankings represent the results of a survey in
October and November, 1973, made by the Institute of Social
Research at The University of Michigan.· A sample of 1,444
Americans participated.

14	Federal Government
2	Colleges and Universities
1	U. S. Military
15	President and Administration
13	Labor Unions
3	Churches and Religious Organizations
12	Local Governments
11	Judicial System — All Courts except Supreme
5	Public Schools
4	Small Businesses
9	U. S. Congress
10	State Government
8	Large Corporations
6	News Media
7	U. S. Supreme Court

Characteristics of a Good Group
Worksheet

1. Please read the list below and rank the following statements that might describe the characteristics of a good group. Place a "1" in front of the statement that is the most important characteristic for a good group, a "2" in front of the next most important characteristic and so on down to the least important, "10". Do this individually first. Do not consult with the others. You have 10 minutes.

Your Rank	Characteristics of a Good Group	Group Rank
_____	Members express freely their negative feelings.	_____
_____	No one in the group digresses from the point.	_____
_____	Members share leadership functions.	_____
_____	Group split into informal subgroups spontaneously.	_____
_____	Goals of the group are explicitly stated at the beginning.	_____
_____	Feelings are considered when tasks are performed.	_____
_____	Leader has a plan for each group meeting.	_____
_____	Members share information freely.	_____
_____	Members avoid conflict situations.	_____
_____	Members who are different are accepted and valued.	_____

2. Now reach consensus as a group as to the most important characteristics. Do not vote. Consensus means everyone agrees at least in part with the decision. List the group's rankings on the right. You have 30 minutes.

Group Observation Check List

Directions: As an observer, place checkmarks in the columns corresponding to the roles you perceive participants playing most often in the group so far.

Names of Group Members	a	b	c	d	e	f	g	h	i	j	k	l

Getting the Job Done Roles (task oriented)

1. Initiator
2. Information giver
3. Information seeker
4. Evaluator
5. Coordinator
6. Clarifier and elaborator

Unifying Roles (people oriented)

7. Encourager
8. Tension breaker/harmonizer
9. Compromiser
10. Follower

Anti-Group Roles

11. Blocker
12. Recognition seeker
13. Dominator
14. Dropout
15. Avoider

Whose participation was most helpful in the group's accomplishment of the task?
What did she do that was helpful?
Whose participation seemed to hinder the group's accomplishment of the task?
What did she do that seemed to hinder?

*Idea from J. William Pfeiffer and John E. Jones, *A Handbook of Structured Experiences for Human Relations Training.* Vol. II. (Iowa City, Iowa: University Associates Press, 1970). p. 78.

exercise thirty-seven: *2 hours*

Group Decision Making   **37**

Purpose: To practice the techniques of decision-making in a
group setting involving group problems.

Making decisions is often a large part of any leadership role.
Decisions can be personal or involve a group such as family,
business organization, committee or agency. Values and
decision-making were discussed elsewhere in this manual in
the context of personal decisions. The same procedures can
be used in making group decisions at an institutional level.

Procedure:

1. Using the worksheet in the section on Decision-Making,
    follow the procedures listed there using a committee,
    departmental or agency problem instead.   For example —

    How to raise money for your agency

    How to train women for managerial positions

    What kind of leave of absence policy to set up
    for your company

    How to cut costs in your agency

    How to get all the household jobs done at home
    when you work all day away from home

2. Discuss with your group how a decision will affect the
    values or priorities of your committee, agency or
    department.

3. Review the brainstorming exercise, page 46. At what
    points in the decision-making process would it be
    suitable to use brainstorming?

4. Develop a plan of action following procedures in the
    Plan of Action exercise, page 51.

exercise thirty-eight: *30 minutes*

38   *Follow the Leader*

Purpose: To have group members give their perceptions of
each other's leadership behavior.

Procedure:

1. Think about how you would rank order each person in
    your group according to how much leadership that person
    has exercised.

2. Without any discussion or talking, each member in turn
    places the other members one behind the other with the
    person showing most leadership at the head and so on
    down the line. Place yourself.

3. If you do not agree with the line-up, move the others
    to where you think they should be. If you do not agree
    with where you are placed, change to a more agreeable
    position.

4. Keep changing the order until all members in the group
    are reconciled to their assigned positions.

Discussion: Do you agree with your Rank Order? How does
the person at the head feel? At the tail? Where did you
rank and why? What criteria did you use in judging where
to place people?

To the Leader:

This exercise can be done periodically during the workshop
in order to measure growth or change in behavior.

Women's Organizations

In this section, we have attempted to gather information on women's organizations that would be helpful to women interested in the goals of this manual. We selected those that are national in scope and are run by and for women. Many of these organizations have local chapters and may be located through telephone directories, or reference librarians in community public libraries.

Additional sources to consult for listings of organizations include:

Women's Rights Almanac, edited by Nancy Gager. Elizabeth Cady Stanton Publishing Company, Bethesda, MD, 1974.

Woman's Almanac: 12 How-To Handbooks in One, compiled and edited by Kathryn Paulson and Ryan A. Kahn. An Armitage Press and Information House Book. Philadelphia and New York, J. B. Lippincott Co., 1976. Refer to the "Woman's Directory," pages 577-624.

Encyclopedia of Associations, volumes 2 and 3, Margaret Fisk, Editor, Detroit, Michigan, Gale Research Co., 1976. (New editions issued regularly.)

Career Guide to Professional Associations: A Directory of Organizations by Occupational Field, compiled and edited by the Staff of The Carroll Press, Cranston, R.I., 1976.

National and International

American Assn. of Univ. Women
2401 Virginia Avenue, NW
Washington, DC 20037

Conducts study/action groups on social, political personal issues, works to mobilize volunteer women power for community service, secure equal opportunities for women in education, industry, government and the professions, increase public awareness of lifestyles and options available to women and in general to promote women in education, international relations cultural interests and the community. Publisher *AAUW Journal,* 5 newspapers, reports on trends in higher education. Access to audio visual materials, and the U.N. grants 100 fellowships for graduate study or post doctoral research. Local chapters may have scholarships for undergraduate students.

Association of Married Women
1206 S. Buchanan Street
Arlington, VA 22204

Gathers information on domestic and family law and customs and discovers ways to overcome the attitude that father knows best.

National Association of Commissions for Women
1249 National Press Bldg.
Washington, DC 20045

Ratification of Equal Rights Amendment. Encourages enforcement of state and federal sex discrimination laws in employment, education, public and community service, taxation, criminal justice, child care, welfare, granting of credit, and coverage of household workers under federal minimum wage. Will help with complaints of sex discrimination. Publishes bimonthly newsletter, "Breakthrough."

National Council of Women of the United States
345 East 46th Street
New York, NY 10017

To serve as an information clearinghouse on women's issues. Publishes bulletin.

National Organization for Women (NOW)
5 South Wabash, Suite 1615
Chicago, IL 60603

Goals include enforcement of equal employment opportunities, revision of state "protective" laws for women, elimination of "sexism" in all levels of education, paid maternity leave, equal fringe benefits, women's right to control own body, etc. Publishes: *NOW Acts* (quarterly), *Do It Now* (monthly newsletter) and pamphlets on NOW'S origins and goals.

Women United
Crystal Plaza 1, Suite 805
2001 Jefferson Davis Highway
Arlington, VA 22202

Since 1971, the organization has worked to promote the Equal Rights Amendment and serve as a clearinghouse for information on ERA topics.

Women's Equity Action League (WEAL)
821 National Press Building
Washington, DC 20045

Goal is to improve the status and lives of all American women. Filed the first complaint of sex discrimination against the academic community. Publishes WEAL Washington Report a monthly newsletter with information on Congressional issues and court actions.

Women's Action Alliance
370 Lexington Avenue
New York, NY 10017

Free, national clearinghouse for information and referral on self-help activities being undertaken by women. Developed *Non-Sexist Child Development Project, Sex Discrimination in State and Local Governments.* Publishes magazine, *Women's Agenda,* information packets on information on sex discrimination in work, organizing multi-services women's centers, how to organize a child care center.

The Gray Panthers
c/o Tabernacle Church
3700 Chestnut Street
Philadelphia, PA 19104

Dedicated to creating a broader range of options for older people. Focuses on ERA, anti-war, health, housing, mass transportation, reforms in social security, court reform, corporate responsibility and political action. Publishes newsletter.

Business and Professions

Credit Women International
2051 Railway Exchange Building
St. Louis, MO 63101

Altrusa International
332 S. Michigan Avenue
Chicago, IL 60604

Goal: To give business and professional women an opportunity to contribute to service work. Concentrates on International Relations, Community Services, Vocational Services. Awards graduate grants to women from Asia and South America and grants for American women in vocational education.

American Business Women's Association (ABWA)
9100 Ward Parkway
Kansas City, MO 64114

Goals: "To elevate the social and business standards of women in business by uniting them nationally for training designed to make them more efficient, considerate, and cooperative toward their work, employees, and clients." Publishes *Women in Business.*

Association for Women in Psychology
243 Russell Rd.
Princeton, NJ 08540

Goals: To end the role which psychology has had in perpetuating unscientific and unquestioned assumptions about the natures of women and men; to encourage unbiased research on sex differences, to establish fact and explode myth, to encourage research and theory directed toward alternative sex-role, child raising practices, life-styles and vocabularies. Publishes *AWP Newsletter,* offers placement service and information on research on women in psychology profession.

Association of Feminist Consultants
222 Rawson Rd.
Brookline, MA 02146

Provides industry, government, educational and non-profit organizations with professional management consulting services aimed at improving the economic and social status of women; to promote the advantages of employing qualified experts on feminist issues.

Federally Employed Women (FEW)
Suite 1249, National Press Building
Washington, DC 20045

Dedicated to take action to end discrimination in employment and in government service. Will assist government employees and applicants who are discriminated because of sex. Publishes FEW's News & Views (newsletter).

Federation of Organizations for Professional Women
1346 Connecticut Ave., NW Rm. 1122
Washington, DC 20036
and
828 Washington St.
Wellesley, MA 02181

Provides a national instrument for information and exchange and concerted action by constituent women's organizations on problems of common interest relating to the advancement of career opportunities for women. The organization is planning to develop a national talent bank. Publications include *Women Today.*

Federation of Women Shareholders in American Business, Inc.
1091 Second Ave.
New York, NY 10009

National Council for Homemaker — Health Aide Services, Inc.
67 Irving Place
New York, NY 10003

Trains homemaker-home health aides to work with families in crisis. Publications: *Homemaker-Service to Strengthen Individual and Family Life; News,* a monthly newsletter for member agencies.

The National Federation of Business and Professional Women's Clubs, Inc.
2012 Massachusetts Avenue, N.W.
Washington, DC 20036

Extends opportunities to business and professional women through education along lines of industrial, scientific, and vocational activities.

Pilot Club International
P.O. Box 4844
Macon, GA 31208

Develops friendship as a means of encouraging and promoting international peace and cultural relations; to inculcate the ideal of service as the basis of all worthy enterprises; to encourage high ethical standards among business and professional women; and to promote active participation in any movement that tends to improve the civic, social, industrial, and commercial welfare of the community. Publications: *The Pilot Log,* a quarterly publication available upon request.

Quota International Inc.
1828 L St., N.W.
Washington, DC 20036

Provides community service to girls and women. The group also provides services for the hearing and speech handicapped. Magazine available upon request.

Soroptimist International of the Americas
1616 Walnut Street
Philadelphia, PA 19103

Adopts programs to increase international understanding and to support the programs of the U.N. Commission of the Status of Men and Women and to extend human rights and opportunities for all. The group emphasizes programs of service to young people. Publications: *The American Soroptimist*, magazine.

Zonta International
59 E. Van Buren
Chicago, IL 60605

Serves the social welfare and educational needs of individual communities and improves the status of women nationally and internationally. Publication: *The Zontian Magazine.*

American Association of University Professors Committee On The Status of Women in the Academic Professions
One Dupont Circle N.W.
Washington, DC 20036

International Association of Physical Education and Sports for Girls and Women (US)
c/o Dr. Edith Betts
University of Idaho
Moscow, ID 83843

Modern Language Association of American Commission on the Status of Women in the Profession
62 Fifth Ave.
New York, NY 10004

National Association of Women Deans, Administrators and Counselors
1028 Connecticut Avenue, N.W.
Washington, DC 20036

American Home Economics Association Home Economists in Business
2010 Mass. Ave., N.W.
Washington, DC 20036

National Association of Women Artists, Inc.
156 Fifth Avenue
New York, NY 10010

Provides an opportunity for members to show their work once a year in a national show and to provide some international exposure.

National League of American Pen Women, Inc.
1300 17th Street N.W.
Washington, DC 20036

Brings together women engaged in creative work of pen, pencil, or brush by promotion and protection of literary, artistic and music production and by promotion and protection of freedom of the press. Publications: *The Pen Woman.*

Women in Communications, Inc.
(Formerly Theta Sigma Phi)
8305-A Shoal Creek Blvd.
Austin, TX 78758

Strives to unite women in all fields of communication and to promote the achievements of women. The group works to combat sex discrimination and provide a national job information service, seminars, clinics, workshops, and some scholarships. Publishes a newsletter and *Matrix*, a magazine

American Newspaper Women's Club, Inc.
1607 22nd Street N.W.
Washington, DC 20008

National Association of Media Women
157 West 126th St.
New York, NY 10027

National Federation of Press Women
312 Cannon Building
Washington, DC 20515

American Medical Women's Association, Inc.
1740 Broadway
New York, NY 10019

The Association has a scholarship loan program for qualified women medical students. It encourages the "appointment of qualified women to policy-making positions in organized medicine," and endorses sex education in the public schools through educational materials. Members receive the *Journal* of the American Medical Women's Association. Also available are "Medicine . . . A Woman's Career," "Medicine Can Be For You," and "Career Choices for Women in Medicine" (vols. I and II).

American Medical Record Association
John Hancock Center, Suite 1850
875 N. Michigan Ave.
Chicago, IL 60611

American Council of Women Chiropractors
3169 S. Grand Blvd.
St. Louis, MO 63118

American Dietetic Association
430 N. Michigan Avenue
Chicago, IL 60611

American Dental Assistants Association, Inc.
211 E. Chicago Avenue
Chicago, IL 60611

American Dental Hygientists Association
211 E. Chicago Avenue
Chicago, IL 60611

American Occupational Therapy Association
6000 Executive Blvd., Suite 200
Rockville, MD 20852

American Physical Therapy Association
1156 15th St., NW
Washington, DC 20005

American Society of Radiologic Technologists
500 N. Michigan Ave., Rm. 836
Chicago, IL 60611

National Federation of Licensed Practical Nurses, Inc.
250 W 57th Street
New York, NY 10019

American Society of Medical Technology
5555 W. Loop St., Suite 200
Bellaire, TX 77401

National League for Nursing
10 Columbus Circle
New York, NY 10019

Association for Women in Mathematics
Wellesley College
Wellesley, MA 02181

Association of Women in Science
1346 Connecticut Ave., NW, Rm. 1122
Washington, DC 20036

National Association of Women Lawyers
American Bar Center
1155 E. 60th Street
Chicago, IL 60637

The following professional organizations have women's caucuses or committees. For easy reference, they have been arranged in alphabetical order by profession rather than by the organization's title. Many circulate job listings information about careers and some provide scholarships.

American Women's Society of Certified Public ACCOUNTANTS
Box 389
Marysville, OH 43040

American Society of Women ACCOUNTANTS
327 S. LaSalle Street
Chicago, IL 60604

American ADVERTISING Federation, Women's Division
1225 Connecticut Avenue, N.W.
Room 200
Washington, DC 20036

National Women's Association of ALLIED BEVERAGE Industries
1300 Pennsylvania Bldg.
Washington, DC 20004

Association of Women in ARCHITECTURE
7440 University Drive
St. Louis, MO 63130

National Association of BANK-WOMEN
111 E. Wacker Drive
Chicago, IL 60601

American Women BUYERS Club
450 Seventh Avenue
New York, NY 10001

National Association of Women in CONSTRUCTION
2800 W. Lancaster Ave.
Fort Worth, TX 76107

COSMETIC Career Women Inc.
614 W. 51st Street
New York, NY 10019

Association of American Women DENTISTS
435 N. Michigan Ave., 17th Flr.
Chicago, IL 60611

Society of Women ENGINEERS
United Engineering Center
345 E. 47th Street
New York, NY 10017

Provides information on the qualification and achievements of women engineers and the opportunities open to them, encourages women to consider an engineering education, serves as a center of information in engineering, provides scholarships for women in engineering.

Society of Women GEOGRAPHERS
1619 New Hampshire Avenue, N.W.
Washington, DC 20009

National Association of Women HIGHWAY SAFETY Leaders
5908 Robin Hood Drive
Upper Marlboro, MD 20870

American HISTORICAL Association Coordinating Committee on Women in the Historical Profession
Eleanor Straub
400 A Street S.E.
Washington, DC 20003

American HOME ECONOMICS Association
2010 Massachusetts Avenue, N.W.
Washington, DC 20036

National Extension HOMEMAKERS Council
Sioux Falls, SD 57101

National Executive HOUSEKEEPERS Association, Inc.
c/o Alberta Wetherholt
Executive Secretary
Room 201, Business and Professional Bldg.
Gallipolis, OH 45631

National Association of INSURANCE Women (International)
1847 E. 15th St.
Tulsa, OK 74104

Academy of MANAGEMENT Committee on the Status of Women in the Management Profession
University of Southern California
Los Angeles, CA 90007

American NURSES Association
2420 Pershing Road
Kansas City, MO 64108

American Association of INDUSTRIAL NURSES
Dorothy M. Saller, R.N.
Executive Director
79 Madison Avenue
New York, NY 10016

National Association for PRACTICAL NURSE Education and Service
Lucille L. Etheridge, R.N.
Executive Director
122 E. 42nd Street
Suite 801
New York, NY 10017

International Association of PERSONNEL Women
2017 Walnut St.
Philadelphia, PA 19103

Ameican Institute of PLANNERS, Women's Rights Committee
1776 Massachusetts Ave., N.W.
Washington, DC 20036

International Association of WOMEN POLICE
6655 N. Avondale Ave.
Chicago, IL 60631

PROFESSIONAL Women's Caucus
P.O. Box 1057
Radio City Station
New York, NY 10019

FASHION Group, Inc.
9 Rockefeller Plaza
New York, NY 10020

Association For Women in PSYCHOLOGY
243 Russell Rd.
Princeton, NJ 08540

American Society for PUBLIC ADMINISTRATION Task Force for Women
1225 Connecticut Avenue, N.W.
Washington, DC 20036

American Women in RADIO AND TELEVISION
1321 Connecticut Avenue, N.W.
Washington, DC 20036

American Council of RAILROAD Women
c/o Anne Armistead
Norfolk & Western Railway Co.
8 N. Jefferson St.
Roanoke, VA 24042

National SECRETARIES Association (International)
2440 Pershing Road
Suite G-10
Kansas City, MO 64108

National Association of EDUCATIONAL SECRETARIES
1801 N. Moore Street
Arlington, VA 22209

National Association of LEGAL SECRETARIES
3005 E. Skelly Dr.,
Suite 120
Tulsa, OK 74105

SOCIOLOGISTS for Women in Society
736 Avondale
Kent, OH 44240

American Society for TRAINING AND DEVELOPMENT
P.O. Box 5307
Madison, WI 53705

Zeta Phi Eta
516 Greenwood Blvd.
Evanston, IL 60201

(Women in speech and communication professions)

Air Line STEWARDS AND STEWARDESSES Association
1329 E St., N.W.
Washington, DC 20004

Education

Delta Kappa Gamma
Society International
P.O. Box 1589
Austin, TX 78767

Unites women educators of the world and advances the professional interest and position of women in education; sponsors and supports desirable educational legislation and initiates legislation in the interests of women educators. Delta Kappa Gamma Monthly News is available on request.

Emma Willard Task Force on Education
University Station
P.O. Box 14229
Minneapolis, MN 55414

Works on methods of eliminating sexism in education; a Task Force book, *Sexism in Education,* provides information and tools for use in the classroom.

Intercollegiate Association of Women Students
P.O. Box 2
2401 Virginia Avenue, N.W.
Washington, DC 20037

Serves as a national voice for women students; works to support legislation to improve the overall status of women in our society. Publications: *Feminine Focus.*

National Association of College Women
c/o Mrs. Lillian Ward McDaniel
417 S. Davis Ave.
Richmond, VA 23220

Promotes fellowship among college women, and studies educational conditions with emphasis upon problems affecting college women; raises educational standards in colleges and universities, stimulates intellectual attainment among college women and arouses in college women a consciousness of their responsibility in aiding in the solution of pertinent problems on local, state and national levels.

National Coalition for Research of Women's Education and Development, Inc.
160 Harper Hall
10th and College Avenue
Claremont, CA 91711

Develops creative solutions to meet the educational needs of women.

Advisory Council on Women's Educational Programs
Suite 821
1832 M Street, N.W.
Washington, DC 20036

The Council welcomes the advice, concerns and experiences of any members of the public as these relate to the progress, problem or injustices suffered by women in the American educational system. Committees: Information Resources: gathers information on the status of women in Education. Legislation "watchdogs" Federal legislation. Federal Policy and Practices examine existing and proposed policies, practices and regulation of federal agencies. Program, analyzes policy matters relating to Women's Educational Equity Act.

Association of American Colleges Project on the Status and Education of Women
1818 R Street N.W.
Washington, DC 20009

Clearinghouse of information concerning women in education and works with institutions, government agencies and other associations and programs affecting women in Higher Education. Publishes monthly newsletter *On Campus With Women* plus research reports, compiles and analyzes laws, announces programs, lists women centers and other information of interest to women.

National Student Association Women's Center
2115 S Street N.W.
Washington, DC 20008

Attempts to identify college and university individuals and groups who have organized models for women's studies programs and projects centered on women's issues.

Phi Chi Theta
718 Judah St.
San Francisco, CA 94122

Provides scholarships in business and economics to qualified and deserving women students.

Family

National Organization to Insure Support Enforcement
12 West 72nd Street
New York, NY 10023

Develops a system of divorce insurance with a provision to convert such insurance into college education or retirement insurance if no divorce occurs. To create effective marital relations laws in general.

Parents Without Partners
7910 Woodmont Avenue
Suite 1000
Washington, DC 20014

Birth Control

Population Association of America
Women Caucus
Prof. Nancy Williamson
Brown University
Providence, RI 02912

Women's National Abortion Action Coalition
156 Fifth Ave.
New York, NY 10010

Since the Supreme Court 1973 decision legalizing abortion, WONAAC has been focusing on the implementation of that decision. Publications: *WONAAC Newsletter.*

Legal Assistance

Human Rights for Women
1128 National Press Building
Washington, DC 20004

Furnishes legal counsel in key discrimination cases; provides for educational and research projects on all aspects of sex prejudice and human and civil rights of women. The organization's directors are leaders in the women's movement. Publications: *Human Rights for Women Newsletter, Job Discrimination Handbook, Law and Women Series,* and a local radio program.

National Organization For Women Legal Defense and Education Fund, Inc.
5 S. Wabash, Suite 1615
Chicago, IL 60603

Provides legal services to bring American women full participation in all phases of life; conducts research on the rights and opportunities available to women. Will provide counsel to women whose civil rights have been infringed.

Women's Equity Action League Legal Defense and Education Fund, Inc.
821 National Press Building
Washington, DC 20005

Research and information; contribute to costs for landmark women's cases; writing proposals for massive legal and educational work; working for enforcement of anti-sex discrimination laws in education. Has a screening committee for legal cases. Future publications in legal and educational areas.

Association of American Law Schools, Women in the Legal Profession
c/o Prof. Mary Wenig
St. Johns Univ. School of Law
Jamaica, NY 11439

American Civil Liberties Union, Women's Rights Project
22 E. 40th Street
New York, NY 10016

Center for Law and Social Policy Women's Rights
1751 N St., N.W.
Washington, DC 20036

Midwest Women's Legal Group
154 W. Randolph St.
Chicago, IL 60601

Racial and Ethnic Minorities

Black Women's Groups

Alpha Kappa Alpha
Alpha Sorority, Inc.
5211 S. Greenwood Avenue
Chicago, IL 60615

Promotes unity and friendship among college women; studies and helps alleviate problems concerning girls and women; and maintains a progressive interest in college life. The organization has scholarship programs for needy women. Publications: *Ivy Leaf.*

Black Women's Community Development Foundation
1028 Connecticut Avenue N.W.
Suite 1010
Washington, DC 20036

Provides   ad hoc and viable women's groups with information about funding, leadership training, analysis of community needs, and other opportunities to enhance the effectiveness of local groups working for social change; to provide direct grants to organizations, institutions and projects that will enable low-income women to serve the needs of their community more effectively.

National Association of Negro Business and Professional Women's Clubs
3411 Lynchester Rd.
Baltimore, MD 21215

Promotes and protects the interests of black professional and businesswomen and "directs their interests toward united action for improved social and civic conditions."

NAACP Legal Defense and Educational Fund
10 Columbus Circle
New York, NY 10019

Spanish-Speaking Women's Groups

National Institute of Spanish-Speaking Women
9841 Airport Blvd.
Suite 1020
Los Angeles, CA 90045

Designed to assist in the development of programs for Spanish-speaking women and to act as an information clearinghouse on Spanish-speaking women.

National Conference of Puerto Rican Women
P.O. Box 4804
Cleveland Park Station
Washington, DC 20008

Obtains for Puerto Rican Women greater participation in the political, economic and social life of the U.S. Publications: A monthly newsletter.

Other Ethnic & Racial Groups

Chinese Women's Association
5432 152nd Street
Flushing, NY 11355

Promotes, stimulates and maintains better understanding of the Chinese and their customs, history and problems and to provide assistance to needy Chinese in Hong Kong and Taiwan. Publications: *The Chinese Woman,* a quarterly for members.

North American Indian Women Association
Box 314
Isleta, NM 87022

Betterment of home, family life and community; Betterment of health and education; Intertribal communication; Awareness of Indian culture; Fellowship among all peoples. Newsletter planned for future.

Slovenian Women's Union
1937 W. Cermak Road
Chicago, IL 60608

Links Slovenian women together and provides them with a single focus and voice. Publications: *Zarja.*

Research

Center for Women Policy Studies
2000 P Street N.W.
Suite 508
Washington, DC 20036

Improves the legal and economic status of American women of all races, cultural backgrounds and economic levels; serves as an advisory and research resource for policy makers in both public and private sectors. Several fact sheets are available: "Women in Unions," "Law Affecting Women in Policing," A Bibliography on Affirmative Action, and "Monograph on Women and Federal Programs."

Feminist Research Center
2490 Channing Way
Berkeley, CA 94704

A collective which sponsors feminist research study groups. The Center has a file of researchers, papers and bibliographies for individuals interested in pursuing feminist research.

Information Center on the Mature Woman
515 Madison Ave.
New York, NY 10022

Functions as a clearinghouse for information on women over 40; provides material for press, speakers, and features for use on radio, television or newspapers on the problems and potential of older women.

International Institute of Sexualidentity
Suite 205-207
Dupont Circle Bldg.
1346 Connecticut Avenue, N.W.
Washington, DC 20036

Collect what is scientifically known about human sexual identity and conceptualizations in all disciplines, collate this information, and disseminate it through scholarly journals, publications, seminars, conferences and television programs. Seeks to serve as a neutral clearinghouse to monitor what is known in the physical sciences about the differences between humans sexually and to use this information as a baseline to examine socially conditioned sexual behavior. No dependence on any government or institution. One major goal: An informed citizenry. Future journal.

International Institute of Women Studies
Suite 205-207
Dupont Circle Bldg.
1346 Connecticut Ave. N.W.
Washington, DC 20036

Advances and encourages research on women's nature and behavior in all disciplines. Publications: *Journal of the International Institute of Women Studies.*

Lucy Stone League
133 E. 58th St.
New York, NY 10022

Conducts research and provides information on the status of women and to work against sex discrimination. Publications: *Lucy Stone,* a biography; *Lucy Stone Five Years After.*

Resource Center on Sex Roles in Education, National Foundation for the Improvement of Education
1201 16th Street N.W.
Washington, DC 20036

Provides technical assistance on women-related studies and conferences at the state or local school levels. Develops and disseminates materials. Serves as a resource network. Represents the Dept. of Education, higher education, and private individuals.

Schlesinger Library on the History of Women in America
3 James Street
Cambridge, MA 02138

Provides to researchers the papers and writings of America's leading women. The library has all the official papers of the National Organization for Women.

International Women's History Archive
2325 Oak Street
Berkeley, CA 94708

Widow's Consultation Center
136 E. 57th Street
New York, NY 10022

Women's History Research Center
2325 Oak Street
Berkeley, CA 94708